THE SPEYSIDE WAY

ABOUT THE AUTHOR

Sandy Anton, a former professor of law, was born near Buckie and spent his early years there and in Fochabers. In his teens he developed a passion for the Scottish hills and their flowers. This interest was not diminished by later scrambles in the Alps in summer and skiing there in winter. When skiing came to Aviemore, he was soon to enjoy long traverses on skis in the Cairngorms and Monadliaths. It was only later that he revived his boyhood interest in picturesque places along the Moray coast and in the country towns and villages along or near to the banks of the Spey. Their history has become his paramount interest.

THE SPEYSIDE WAY

by

SANDY ANTON

CICERONE PRESS
2 POLICE SQUARE, MILNTHORPE, CUMBRIA, LA7 7PY
www.cicerone.co.uk

ISBN 1 85284 331 4

G. F. Robson colour etching is reproduced by permission of Aberdeen University. P. F. Anson watercolours are reproduced with acknowledgement to Moray Council Museums Service.

ACKNOWLEDGEMENTS

The author thanks friends who joined with him in exploring Speyside, in particular James Innes and Len and Judy Harvey. He has been helped by the expertise of Jim Strachan, the Manager of the Speyside Way, and by the kindness of so many people on the route. He is especially grateful to Dennis Malcolm of the Balmenach Distillery, for reading the appendix to this book and for encouraging its inclusion. He owes much to the staff of other distilleries, notably of Cardhu, Dailuaine and Knockdhu. Not least, he appreciates the helpful advice and the work of the Cicerone team in publishing the book.

Advice to Readers

Readers are advised that while every effort is taken by the author to ensure the accuracy of this guidebook, changes can occur which may affect the contents. It is advisable to check locally on transport, accommodation, shops, etc, and readers should note that forestry operations or landfalls may cause the standard route to be closed.

The publisher would welcome notes of any such changes.

Front cover: Along the River Avon to Ben Avon

CONTENTS

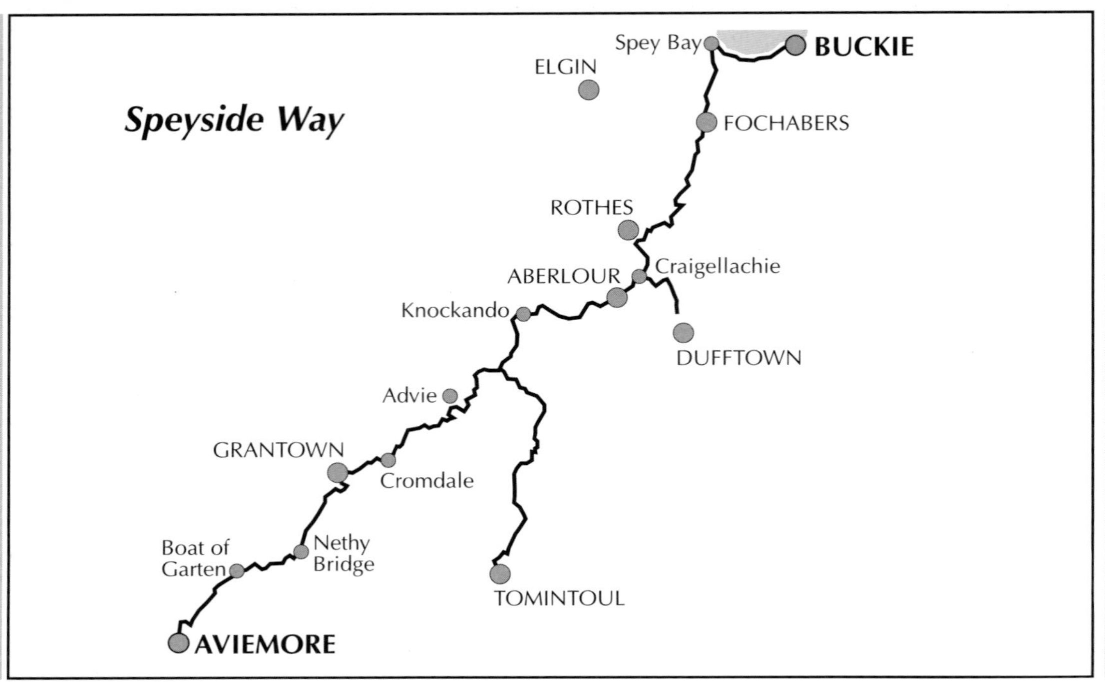
Speyside Way
Spey Bay
BUCKIE
ELGIN
FOCHABERS
ROTHES
Craigellachie
ABERLOUR
Knockando
DUFFTOWN
Advie
GRANTOWN
Cromdale
Boat of Garten
Nethy Bridge
TOMINTOUL
AVIEMORE

Map Key

- Main road
- Minor road
- Railway, station
- Dismantled railway
- Speyside Way on a road
- .. on a track
- .. on a path
- Loch
- Wide river
- River
- Car park
- Viewpoint
- Tourist attraction
- Tourist information
- Distillery
- Youth hostel
- Caravan site
- Camp site
- Settlement
- Woodland

Pictish stone at Arndilly (Chapter 5)

CHAPTER 1

INTRODUCTION

Speyside is one of the lovelier parts of the British Isles. It is overlooked by some of its highest mountains, Cairngorm (4084ft), Braeriach (4208ft) and Sgoran Dubh Mor (3658ft), which often carry snow in their corries as late as June. Beneath them are some of Scotland's grandest pine forests. These circle round from Glen Feshie, past Inschriach and Rothiemurchus, to Glenmore, and, with the Abernethy Forest crossing the River Spey near Grantown, the visitor can enjoy a woodland wonderland unique in Europe. While the larger picture is of pine forests, they are not unmixed with attractive birch woods, with juniper, willows and a ground cover of heather, bilberry and crowberry, ferns, moor grass and cotton grass. In the woods are many animals and birds uncommon in the rest of the UK: there are red deer, roe deer, red squirrels and wild cats, and there are birds too numerous to mention, though including eagles, osprey, capercaillie and crested tits. Then there is the River Spey itself, for much of the route the fastest and clearest of Scotland's larger rivers. With its banks lined with alders, willows, rowans and other trees, its sparkling waters make a dazzling foreground to memorable pictures. It is little wonder that Scottish Natural Heritage (SNH) in February 1999 advised the Scottish Parliament that the creation of a national park in the general area of the Cairngorms would be appropriate. This advice has been accepted, and consideration of the detailed scheme is proceeding. Whatever the final scheme, a considerable part of the Speyside Way is likely to fall within the boundaries of the park.

The Speyside Way runs from Buckpool, near the mouth of the Spey, for a distance of some 80 miles, to Aviemore. It may

Salmon being landed near Spey Bay (Chapter 2)

be walked or cycled in either direction, though, while the cyclist may prefer to travel northwards to take advantage of the fall in the ground, the walker may wish to go southwards to be in better training for the more difficult sections towards the south. If, however, the 'spur' to Tomintoul is left aside, Aviemore is only some 200m above sea level, so that, on the whole, the walking is not tough. An exception is the Tomintoul spur, where the height gained is over 600m and where, in winter snows, the walker should be well equipped. The route is well signposted and, throughout this book, the term 'Speyside Way Sign' is contracted to SWS. Rather than relying on signposting alone, however, it is always better to carry a map (see below) and to know how to use it.

How to use this Guide

This Guide is in two parts. The Introduction describes the origins of the Speyside Way and refers to its objectives. It outlines the general nature of the route following the valley of the Spey, from its mouth to Aviemore, through one of the more unspoilt and beautiful parts of Scotland. The Guide introduces the reader to the history and natural history of this route. It refers to Speyside's agriculture, industry and sport, and emphasises the importance of the former Speyside line, whose trackbed the Way so often utilised. The latter part of the Introduction gives practical advice to users of the Way, whether walkers or cyclists, on such matters as transport to its starting points and, within the route, accommodation, and addresses and telephone numbers which may prove useful in accessing information.

The following ten chapters of the Guide describe the Way from Buckie to Aviemore in more detail. Each chapter is accompanied by a section from the official Harvey's Speyside Way map (1:40,000). It is assumed that, in addition to using the signposting and waymarking of the route, people will be equipped either with the official map or the Ordnance Survey Landranger

1:50,000 maps numbers 28 and 36, and will seldom need assistance in finding the route. The Guide occasionally offers such assistance, but concentrates rather upon drawing the reader's attention to matters, perhaps familiar to locals, which add interest to the journey for visitors. These chapters also mention places and objects adjacent to the Way which are well worth a visit.

The route description is not divided into daily sections, because walkers and cyclists have different tastes and capacities. A cyclist could easily cover the whole route in a couple of days. Though some guidance is given in the following chapters, part of the fun of doing a route like this is in the planning. Readers should note that parts of the route are in unfrequented country where, apart from in the larger towns and villages, shops are rare. These villages include – south to north – Aviemore, Boat of Garten, Nethy Bridge, Grantown-on-Spey, Tomintoul, Ballindalloch, Aberlour, Craigellachie, Dufftown, Fochabers, Garmouth and Buckie. Finally, there are lots of interesting places to see and things to do en route. Take plenty of time: it will be worth it!

Speyside, more than anywhere else, is the home of the Scottish malt whisky industry. The Appendix contains a brief introduction to the growth of the industry on Speyside, refers to some of the distilleries near the Speyside Way which are open to visitors, describes how malt whiskies are made there, and ends with an 'Early Learning' introduction to the pleasant task of sampling them.

THE SPEYSIDE WAY

The Speyside Way differs from some long-distance walking routes in the sense that it is not primarily a test of physical endurance. The plan originally canvassed by the then Countryside Commission for Scotland entailed a walk through Glen Tilt, over the Lairig Ghru to Glenmore, and from there down Speyside to Spey Bay. This route would have been an exciting one and quite a test of stamina, but was criticised by many experienced climbers as being potentially dangerous in winter for the less experienced. This argument won the day, a result not unassisted by difficulties encountered in securing wayleaves in the section from Glenmore to Ballindalloch. Undeterred, the Countryside Commission and Moray District Council went ahead and devised a route from Ballindalloch to Spey Bay, with two interesting but quite different 'spurs' to Dufftown and Tomintoul. This route was opened in 1981 and, though it does not quite conform to the Countryside Commission's original criteria for the length of a long-distance route, it has proved popular and successful in practice. The Secretary of State for Scotland approved of a submission by Scottish Natural Heritage for extending the route from Spey Bay to Buckie and from Ballindalloch to Aviemore. The necessary finance was made available and the route was opened on 8th April 2000.

The justification for the extended route is less its physical challenge than that of offering an introduction to one of the most beautiful and interesting parts of Scotland. The recognition of this lies behind the recently announced intention of the Government to designate the River Spey as a Special Area of Conservation. It is a place where history and natural history, agriculture and industry, tourism and sports – new and old – come together in a quite unique way. In the lower part of Speyside the accent is on arable farming and grain crops, especially barley, though there is market gardening and fruit growing to meet local needs, including those of Baxters of Fochabers. Towards the central part the accent is rather upon stock rearing, but barley remains a traditional crop, still meeting some of the demands of the malt whisky distilleries for which Speyside is famous. In the upper part of the route, the accent is on sheep farming and tourism. Agriculture serves local industry, and the distilleries, which are central to local industry, in turn assist

Dr Grant's statue in Tomiintoul Square (Chapter 9)

tourism. The highly publicised 'Whisky Trail' attracts tourists from far and near to the distillery visitor centres which offer such a pleasant and warming welcome. Tourism came to Speyside with the railways and, without them, places like Nethy Bridge, Carr Bridge, Boat of Garten and Grantown-on-Spey could not have developed as they have today.

The Victorians were keen walkers and 'pedestrianism' was a sport in its own right. But the more affluent came to Speyside also for the excellent salmon and sea trout fishing and some for grouse shooting and deer stalking. Downhill skiing became popular near Aviemore in the 1960s with the opening of the ski tows on Cairngorm. On a clear spring day more than 5000 people, young and not so young, can enjoy descents of 1500ft/450m on Cairngorm. For the adventurous there is gliding near Aviemore and watersports of all kinds at Loch Inch, a little south of Aviemore. There is much to see and much to do along this rather special route, the Speyside Way. Those walking or cycling it need not be hurried: they can take time to stroll round the old villages and, perhaps especially, to pause at the bridges and at breaks in the trees to view the changing moods of the river. The river, as the place names often suggest, for long dominated life in the area: it is still a feature central to the Way. But the walk may also be an opportunity for viewing the local animal and plant life: it is rich and varied. Particularly on summer evenings sightings of roe deer and red squirrels are not uncommon. Sightings of birds depend on the place and season, but there may be tits, including the rare crested tit, wrens, pied woodpeckers and dippers. There may be a variety of ducks, and the upper part of the route offers a fair chance of ospreys being seen before their departure for warmer climes. The river banks are marked out by silver birch, hazel and alder. Along the track there are beech, gean, juniper and rowan and there may be blaeberries, rasps and brambles for hunter-gatherers. There are many places of historical interest: there are several enigmatic relics of the Picts. There are castles to be visited, though fewer than in Deeside or Donside. In Ballindalloch Castle, however, we have the very epitome of such a Scottish castle.

The Speyside Way, as now extended, may be walked in either a northerly or southerly direction; the Ranger Service suggets a southerly direction starting near the mouth of the river and, with the diversions or 'spurs' to Dufftown and Tomintoul, ending at Aviemore. The journey starts a few miles to the east of the Spey at Buckie and, after visiting Spey Bay, follows country paths near the river to Fochabers. After passing that formerly sleepy village, the Way joins a quiet road high above the Spey to Boat o'Brig, a road affording attractive views over the Laich of Moray. From Boat o'Brig the Way moves upwards largely on forestry paths along the west side of Ben Aigan before descending on an unfrequented road towards Craigellachie. In the days of the Speyside Railway, Craigellachie was known as 'Craigellachie Junction' since railway lines there radiated in three different directions. The central portion of the Way, from Craigellachie to Nethy Bridge, apart from the hilly 'spur' from Ballindalloch to Tomintoul, makes considerable use of the trackbed of the former Speyside line which, for many visitors, will seem a characteristic of the Way. The old railway closely followed the River Spey, and the journey along it by train must have been as enjoyable in the past for its passengers as it is today for walkers and cyclists. Above all, Speyside is the heartland of the malt whisky industry and several distilleries are situated either close to the Speyside Way, or within walking distance of it. The book concludes with an Appendix on Speyside malt whisky.

The generally gentle gradients of the Speyside Way make it an attractive route for the cyclists who frequent it. They are made welcome except on the off-road sections between Ballindalloch and Tomintoul and on the official parts of the route between Ballindalloch and Cromdale. They may, of course, choose to use such public roads as the B9008 to Tomintoul or, as an interesting variant, the B9136 up Glen Avon

Entering Speyside from Huntly

until it meets the A939 from Grantown to Tomintoul. They may also use the secondary road – the B9102 – from Mains of Dalvey via Wester Rynaballoch to Cromdale. Cyclists, again, are requested to use the B9104 between Speybay and Fochabers rather than the Way itself.

The use of horses is apparently permitted on such sections of the Speyside Way as use the railway trackbed between Craigellachie and Ballindalloch, but it is suggested that intending riders should contact the Ranger Service (see below) for up-to-date advice.

How to get there

Transport

There are many points of access to the Speyside Way, but it may be conveniently reached by travellers from afar by air or rail.

TO COMMENCE AT BUCKIE

From Aberdeen Railway Station take a train to Keith from where a bus service is available to Buckie. Going by air to Aberdeen Airport, trains to Keith may be reached at Dyce Station, close to Aberdeen Airport. For enquiries as to rail fares and times tel. 08457 484950 (national rail enquiries) or 08457 6015939 (Scotrail), or visit www.scotrail.co.uk. Going by air to Inverness Airport, buses are available at Inverness using StageCoach/ Bluebird to Buckie, changing at Elgin. The service is not infrequent. For enquiries as to bus fares and times, contact StageCoach/Bluebird, tel. 01463 239292.

TO COMMENCE AT AVIEMORE

Take the Inverness train from the south and alight at Aviemore (see above for Scotrail phone enquiries). If travelling to Inverness by air, Citylink offers a service from Inverness (Farraline Park Bus Station) to Aviemore. Citylink also has a bus service from Edinburgh to Aviemore via Perth, tel. 0870 5505050 (lines open 8am to 8pm) or visit www.citylink.co.uk. Highland Country Buses offer a service from Inverness Bus Station to Aviemore, Grantown-on-Spey, Nethy Bridge and vice versa, tel. (Inverness) 01463 222244 or (Aviemore) 01479 811211.

For buses operating near the Speyside Way, Stagecoach/ Bluebird publish a Moray Area Timetable, tel. Aberdeen 01224 212266 or Elgin 01343 544222. Highland Country Buses, as stated above, offer a service from Inverness Bus Station to and from Aviemore, Grantown-on-Spey and Nethy Bridge, tel. (Inverness) 01463 222244 or (Aviemore) 01479 811211.

WALKING IN

There will be some for whom the Speyside Way in its 'official' form may not be sufficiently long or tough and strenuous. There is no real problem here. The experienced hillwalker may take a car or train to Blair Atholl and from there walk through Glen

Tilt as far as the White Bridge over the River Dee. If feeling energetic, walkers may then continue their journey over the Lairig Ghru, though taking account of the fact that there is no accommodation – apart from Corrour Bothy – before reaching Coylum Bridge or traversing the Chalamain Gap to Glenmore Youth Hostel. From Glenmore it is only some 5.5 miles/9km to Aviemore. This, however, is a serious option only for the very fit and the well-equipped. There is a saying among lovers of the area that *'It may be winter any day in the Cairngorms'*. If you choose not to walk the Lairig Ghru you may descend upon Inverey Youth Hostel to spend the night before resuming your journey to Speyside. As an alternative to the Lairig Ghru you may walk the Lairig an Laoigh, but both these routes are some 28 miles/45km in length. An alternative route, some 18.5 miles/ 30km, is to go past Braemar to Invercauld, and from there to take the Bealach Dearg route to the col to the west of Culardoch, dropping down to Loch Builg, thence to lower Glen Avon, Delnabo and Tomintoul. This takes the walker or cyclist through interesting and unfrequented places, though it does not go directly to Aviemore. All these routes are well described in *Scottish Hill Tracks* (1999), published by the Scottish Rights of Way Society, 24 Annandale Street, Edinburgh EH7 4AN.

TAXIS

These are relatively rare in the remoter parts of Scotland. It is worth remembering that some of the B&Bs on or near the Way may be prepared to assist with transport arrangements but it is essential to do this at the time of booking. For obtaining taxis the following numbers may be useful:

Buckie – tel. 01542 832084; 01542 833352
Craigellachie – tel. 01340 881352
Fochabers – tel. 01343 820820; 01343 820538
Dufftown – tel. 01340 820718
Aberlour – tel. 01340 871416

Grantown-on-Spey – tel. 01479 872160; 01479 873443
Aviemore – tel. 01479 810141; 01479 811111

ACCOMMODATION

A list of accommodation available on or near the Way is published by the Moray Council Ranger Service and is available at several tourist offices. At holiday times it is advisable to book in advance. There are youth hostels at Tomintoul, tel. 01807 580280 and Aviemore, tel. 01479 810345.

TOURIST OFFICES

Aberdeen: 23 Union Street (opposite Broad Street), Aberdeen, tel. 01224 288828 (Jan–Dec)

Aviemore: Grampian Road, Aviemore, Inverness-shire PH22 1PP, tel. 01479 810363 (Jan–Dec). Brochure line tel. 01426 983420

Buckie: Buckie Library, Cluny Place, tel. 01542 832121 (May–Sept)

Dufftown: Clock Tower, The Square, Dufftown, tel. 01340 829501 (Apr–Oct)

Elgin: 17 High Street, Elgin IV30 1EG, tel. 01343 542666; 01343 543388 (Jan–Dec)

Grantown-on-Spey: High Street, Grantown-on Spey, Morayshire, tel. 01479 872773 (Apr–Oct)

Keith: Church Road, Keith, tel. 01542 882634 (May–Sept)

Tomintoul: The Square, Tomintoul, tel. 01807 580285 (Apr–Oct)

WEBSITE AND RANGER SERVICES

www.speysideway.org This is well worth visiting, and, notably, gives advice relating to recent route deviations because of forestry operations and any recent closures for other reasons.

The Route Manager, Speyside Way, Boat of Fiddich, Craigellachie AB38 9RQ, tel. 01340 881266 (ansafone)

Andrew Wells, Estate Ranger, Glenlivet Estate Office, Main Street, Tomintoul AB37 9EX, tel. 01807 580283, fax 580319. An excellent map of paths near Tomintoul, including the route of the Speyside Way near Tomintoul, is available from the Estate Office.

Forestry Commission Recreation Manager, The Forest Office, Balnacoul, Fochabers IV32 7LL, tel. 01343 820223. The Commission publishes a map of forests in Moray and Deveron, including some adjacent to the Speyside Way.

Moray Council Coastal Ranger Service, Council Headquarters, High Street, Elgin IV30 1BX, tel. 01343 56349.

MAPS

An official map for the Speyside Way has been produced, in partnership with Moray and Highland District Councils, by Harvey, 12–22 Main Street, Doune, Perthshire FK16 6BJ, tel. 01786 841202. The scale is normally 1:40,000, though higher in the village maps. It is highly recommended.

The Ordnance Survey Landranger 1:50,000 maps, Sheets 28 and 36, are useful.

DISTANCES (INCLUDING 'SPURS')

	miles	km
Buckpool Harbour to Tugnet	4.0	6.4
Garmouth to Fochabers	4.4	7.1
Fochabers to Craigellachie	12.5	20.1
Craigellachie to Dufftown	4.0	6.4
Craigellachie to Knockando	6.4	10.4
Knockando to Ballindalloch	4.3	7.0
Ballindalloch to Tomintoul	15.0	24.2
Ballindalloch to Grantown-on-Spey	13.0	20.9
Grantown-on-Spey to Nethy Bridge	6.0	9.6
Nethy Bridge to Aviemore	11.0	17.5
Approximate total	**80.6**	**130**

The suggested walk to Garmouth and Kingston would add some 3.4 miles (5.5km).

CHAPTER 2

BUCKIE TO SPEY BAY

Starting point:	**Buckpool Harbour**
Distance:	**4 miles/6.4km**
Height gained/lost:	**None**
Time required:	**2–3 hours**
Car parking:	**At starting point, Spey Bay and Tugnet**
Facilities:	**Wide range at Buckie, pub at Buckpool, pub food at Portgordon, hotel at Spey Bay, cafe and toilets at Tugnet**

Summary of route

The new starting point of the Speyside Way is the former harbour of the village of Buckpool, now a part of Buckie. The harbour itself has been filled in and has become a recreation and car park, though the north-west harbour wall remains, seemingly impervious to every storm. There are as yet no toilet facilities there, and for provisions it would be better to make the short journey to Buckie. Move east across the Buckie Burn towards the Yardie – old, painted fisher-houses, gable end to sea – and move upwards east of the Buckie Burn. Go left at Mid Street, meeting Cluny Terrace and Cluny Place. Just before Cluny Place meets a main street, West Church Street, a building containing the local library, museum and art gallery is to be seen on the right. This now holds the tourist office (tel. 01542 832121). The town of Buckie possesses ample accommodation of every kind. It has an abundance of shops and sporting facilities, including golf courses to the west at Buckpool and to the east at Strathlene.

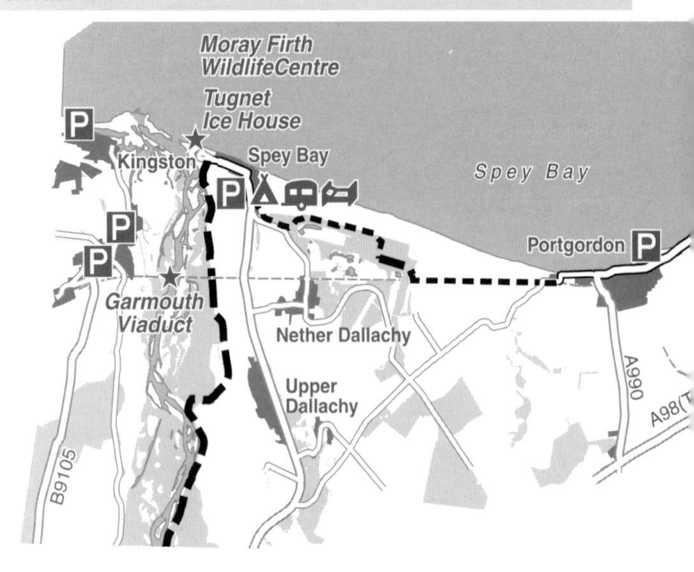

The Speyside Way is signposted at Buckpool Harbour and, going west, the Way soon turns first left and first right to follow the pavement on the north side of the A990 towards Portgordon. Soon Buckpool is left and rough grasses cover the land between the pavement and a partially protected shore. From here, the long shoreline to the west appears and Lossiemouth rises out of the sea as a significant promontory. Further west, the coastline from Brora and Helmsdale to Wick comes into view. This is a place of fine cloudscapes and often of spectacular sunsets. On the left the track of the old Great North of Scotland Railway (GNSR) may often be seen and midway to Portgordon it crosses the Gollachy Burn by a striking GNSR bridge. Shortly, Portgordon village is entered and its spick-and-span fisher-houses catch the eye. There is a modest village square, where the Richmond Arms offers bar lunches.

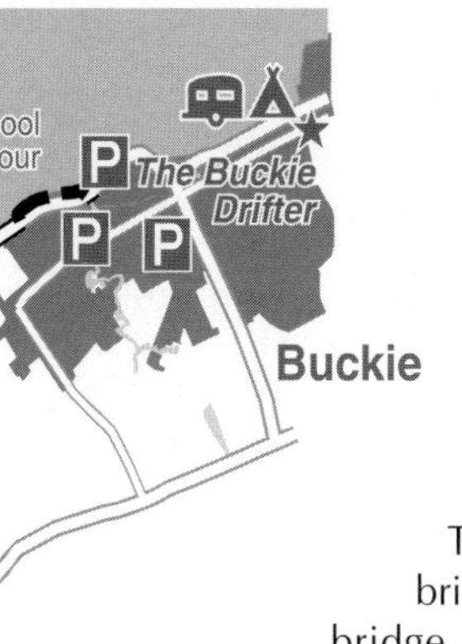

At the west end of Portgordon the A990 takes a sharp turn southwards and is followed for few yards by the Speyside Way until Way signposts (SWS) show that the route is to be followed past a gate to the trackbed of the old railway. This heads directly west, crossing the Tynet Burn by a recently constructed bridge and another burn by an old stone bridge. Finally the Way comes to a railway bridge formerly serving Lower Auchenreath Farm.

Here the Way leaves the old rail track and turns first right (SWS) and then left (SWS) into a forestry clearing. A SWS sign soon points to a rough woodland track, well marked, which on the south side follows, first the Spey Bay golf course and then a 'driving range'. The track meets the Spey Bay to Fochabers Road (B9104) near an old water tower. From here, turning right, it is no distance to Spey Bay (where there is a hotel) or Tugnet (where there is a Wild Life Centre, with a cafe, a collection of artefacts and toilets).

BUCKPOOL: Buckpool has been a fishing village since the 18th century. For a long time the boats were simply hauled up upon the shingle shore by men and women. There was no harbour until one was built there in 1857 by Sir Robert Gordon of Letterfourie. But the harbour silted up too easily: in north-east gales the breakers brought in sand and shingle and the harbour was gradually abandoned by fishermen. The outer sea-wall of the harbour remains, a tribute to the skills of the engineers who made it. Its basins, now filled in, have become a recreation park.

As you walk along the coast road to the west from Buckpool your ears are assailed by the shrill calls of the seagulls and perhaps of curlews, oyster catchers and ringed and golden plovers. Seals frequent the beach when the protective boulders allow it. There were formerly stake-nets for salmon near the shore, a disused salmon fishing bothy and, nearer the track, an old ice house dating from 1834. Until the 1950s salmon were taken from the nets at first light, wrapped in reeds, placed in wooden boxes and covered with ice, before being taken to Buckpool Station to meet the then daily fish train to catch the next day's market at Billingsgate.

BUCKIE: Buckpool is now part of Buckie, an amalgam of several fishing villages including Yardie (now a preservation area), Ianston, Gordonburgh and Portessie. These lay near the shore where the fishermen formerly chose to live to be close to their boats. Their houses still remain, often with their gable ends facing the sea, to give some protection from the cold north winds, many of them quaintly huddled together and often brightly painted. Latterly in the 19th century, quite gradually, a species of linear town was developed on the ridge above these shores. Here Buckie's East and West Church Streets were developed to cater for business, shopping and other urban facilities which the increasing prosperity of the fishing villages required. But many fishermen continued to perish at sea in the absence of suitable shelter and there was a constant call for a harbour of refuge. This was eventually built to the east as Cluny Harbour, and Buckpool Harbour became redundant.

Buckie still remains essentially a fishing port though the focus of its activities has changed from herring to white fishing and, more recently, to the catching and preparation of shellfish. There are still shipbuilding yards at Buckie which, apart from fishing boats and fine yachts, have built one or two impressive sailing ships. Buckie possesses an excellent Maritime Heritage Centre (The Buckie Drifter, tel. 01542 834645) tracing the development of fishing boats from the open-decked sailing boats, the 'scaffies' of the 18th and early 19th centuries, to the 'fifies' and the 'zulus' of the late 19th century, to the steam drifters of the early 20th century and to the seine net boats of the 1930s and later. These last have become the workhorses of Buckie fishing today. The Heritage Centre also possesses a 1920s style steam drifter, a pensioned-off lifeboat, and books from the Peter F Anson collection of maritime art. Still more interesting, however, are the modern, and skilfully presented, computer and video descriptions of the life of the herring, its time and place of spawning, its feeding grounds and feed, and its natural enemies. The centre also offers harbour tours to illustrate the work of netmakers, boatbuilders and fish processors.

PORTGORDON: Though there were earlier fishers here, the 'official' founding of Portgordon goes back to 1797 when the fourth Duke of Gordon provided funds for the building of better boats and, in 1874, caused the harbour to be built. It became quite important for fishing, for the fitting out of ships for Garmouth and even for the trading of grain for coal and salt. But the harbour was a small one and, with the building of Cluny Harbour at Buckie and the coming there of steam drifters, Portgordon Harbour fell into decline. It is now home to a few pleasure boats and boats used to lay creels for crab and lobster fishing.

Portgordon Station hardly seems a likely starting point for an exciting spy story, and a true one at that. It is well told by Eric Simpson in his *Discovering Banff, Moray and Nairn* (Edinburgh, 1992, p179). It was wartime and on 30th September 1940 the station's porter and stationmaster had suspicions about two prospective passengers. It was not only that the lady was more attractive and the man more smooth than those usually arriving in Portgordon station at 7.30 on a Monday morning, but they seemed to have come from nowhere and both had wet feet. The stationmaster alerted the local bobby who in turn alerted Mr Simpson's father, the Buckie police inspector. From then on the scenario was that of an alert and intelligent policing action. It appeared that another male spy had landed near Portgordon. He had travelled to Buckie and from there to Edinburgh, where he was arrested. The two male spies were tried and executed. The lady was not tried, and her subsequent history remains obscure.

CHAPTER 3

SPEY BAY AND GARMOUTH

Starting point:	**Tugnet**
Distance:	**Official route 1 mile/1.5km. Deviation to Garmouth and Kingston adds 4.5 miles/7km**
Height gained/lost:	**Insignificant**
Time required:	**Official route 30 minutes; with deviation 3 hours**
Car parking:	**At Spey Bay, Tugnet and Garmouth**
Facilities:	**Hotel at Spey Bay, cafe and toilets at Tugnet, hotel and shops at Garmouth**
Transport:	**Occasional buses to/from Elgin**

SUMMARY OF 'OFFICIAL' ROUTE

This description is brief since it is intended to cover only the route from Tugnet to the point where it meets the track of the former GNSR railway. This is on the view that most walkers will seize the chance to visit the old-world villages of Garmouth and Kingston. Some knowledge of their past helps materially to understand the history of Speyside as a whole.

The Speyside Way formerly commenced at Tugnet or Spey Bay, rather than the western side of the river, possibly because there were and are convenient riverside farm or fishers' tracks to speed walkers or cyclists on their way towards Fochabers. The route starts at the old Tugnet Ice House (see below). Pass it and the Moray Firth Wild Life Centre (which offers light refreshments and toilet facilities) on their south side following SWS for some 150m and then take a farm track to the right (SWS) for about half a mile to a point where signs to the GNSR bridge (see below) appear. Then go to the right either by the elevated rail track or by the nearby cycle track to the bridge. Having crossed the bridge, an elevated causeway passes above Garmouth golf course and after this the track may be left either at the first or second road bridge over the former railway. Near the second there is a small car park and picnic area and you are already in Garmouth. Here there is a small supermarket, a post office, and a hotel offering bar lunches.

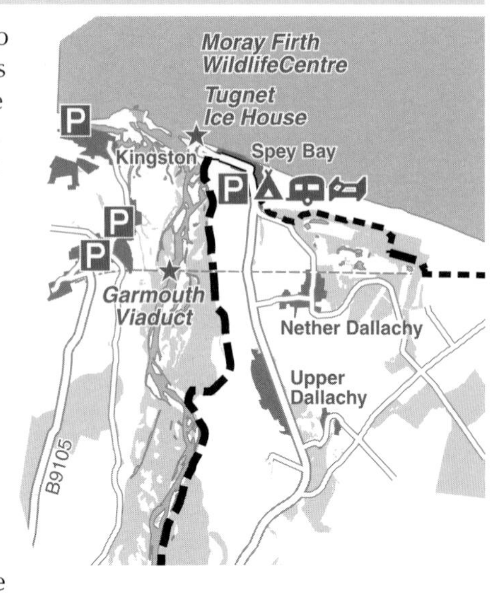

SPEY BAY AND TUGNET: Whatever the wish to get going quickly, time should be taken to walk along the pebbled shore and to savour the views across the Moray Firth to Tarbat Ness, Morven Hill and Caithness. To the east can be seen the Bin Hill of Cullen – itself a notable viewpoint – and to the south Ben Aigan, Ben Rinnes and other hills dominating the Speyside Way. The beach here has a rich variety of stones brought down from every part of Speyside. The visitor is greeted by the shrill calls of seabirds and may be rewarded with sightings of cormorants, curlews, gulls, fulmars, sandpipers, kittiwakes and ringed plovers. These are but a foretaste of the sightings to be enjoyed in the ever changing estuary of the Spey. The car park at Tugnet has various notices from the Scottish Wild Life Trust illustrating the many birds and marine creatures to be seen from here. Across the river are the villages of Garmouth (to the left) and Kingston (to the right). But the meeting of the waters of the Spey with the sea is interesting in itself.

The Spey is an extremely rapid river and, especially in flood, carries down an immense quantity of sand and stones towards the sea. But the velocity of the water is rapidly reduced when it meets the sea and the river releases quickly its heavier elements. Since the sea has normally a westerly drift, a stone and shingle spit is gradually formed west of Tugnet. This in turn tends to erode the river bank at the western or Kingston side. When the water is low the last mile or so of the river looks peaceful enough with its sinuous streams and small islands. When it is high, however, the turbulent flow of the river is awe-inspiring.

OLD ICE HOUSE: At Tugnet visits to the old ice house and Moray Firth Wildlife Visitor Centre are recommended. The former was built in 1830 and is one of the finest of its kind. It goes back to the days when the Dukes of Gordon, later of Richmond and Gordon, had immensely valuable fishing rights, both at the mouth of the river and upwards for some nine miles. They leased these to two entrepreneurs, Messrs Gordon and Richardson, for £1500 per annum, an immense sum in those days. They employed some 130 men who assisted in catching the salmon and exporting it to London and elsewhere. In the days before the manufacture of ice, winter ice was collected (or imported from Norway), stored in buildings insulated by feet of earth and used to preserve the salmon until they could be marketed. In spring the fish were packed in ice and usually sent by sea to London. As summer approached, reverting to an earlier practice, they were boiled in vinegar – the boilers currently being exhibited in the Wildlife Centre – packed in barrels containing some 36 pounds of salmon and sent to London or salted and sent overseas. Once the GNSR reached

The old ice houses at Tugnet

the Spey in 1886, the Fochabers-on-Spey Station was available to transport the fish by rail as far as Billingsgate. Though it is still possible to visit the ice house, it was flooded in the spring of 2000 and some of its former exhibits are no longer displayed there. Until a decision is reached on its future, the exhibits are being looked after by the Moray Firth Wildlife Centre. This, and its café, may be closed in the winter months.

Until the 1940s there was salmon fishing from Tugnet in the Spey estuary and a building remains where the fishers were housed. Behind it are one or two of the old salmon cobles; another is in the ice house. The cobles were rowed upstream and the net released to effect a broad sweep across the river. The coble would return to the shore and the men would haul in the net, decanting their catch of shiny and glittering, light blue salmon on to the shore, wriggling about in protest, soon to be stunned by the fishers. Today, however, this commercial fishery at Tugnet has been abandoned in favour of rod fishing.

P. F. Anson's watercolour of Buckpool harbour (Chapter 2)

Seine net boat in Buckie harbour by P. F. Anson (Chapter 2)

Buckie boats in Buckie harbour (Chapter 2)

GARMOUTH VIADUCT: This lies about half a mile south of Spey Bay near the site of the former Fochabers-on-Spey Station of the GNSR. This station, and with it the line from Cullen to Elgin, fell a victim to Dr Beeching's axe in 1968. So now the walker who wishes to visit Garmouth and Kingston may follow the old track of the line westwards over the viaduct. Built in 1886, this bridge in former days took the railway to Garmouth and on to Elgin. Coming from the east the old rail track now follows a long man-made causeway past attractive birches, until the first embattled circular supports for the main span are reached. This span is an impressive 350ft/107m in length and some 40ft/12m in height. A wooden walkway replaces the rails and, while crossing the bridge, you are torn between the unfolding views down and up the valley and the elegant patterns of the girders on the main span. Leaving the bridge, an elevated causeway may be left either at the first or second road bridge over the former railway. Near the second there is a small car park and picnic area and you are already in Garmouth.

GARMOUTH AND KINGSTON: Much history attaches to these old-world villages. Garmouth was officially created in 1587 but entered the history books only with the landing of Charles II (the Merry Monarch) in June 1650 when he signed – under coercion as he claimed – the Solemn League and Covenant. Unlike some of the villages higher up the Spey, Garmouth was not a 'planned settlement'. It is in fact gloriously unplanned, with narrow twisting streets. An early writer says:

> *'...but there is no such thing as a straight street in the place: no trace of an architect has been here to drill the old houses into regimental regularity'.*

In former times the houses were built with whatever materials were near to hand, in this case stones for the foundations and a few feet higher. Above this the walls were made of clay strengthened with straw. But they were well harled with rough cast and kept out the weather for many a year. Garmouth today has not the variety of tradesmen it had in the past, as it now seems unlikely to have tailors, milliners, founders, block and tackle makers and wood merchants. But the old Star Inn is still there in the guise of the Garmouth Hotel, still offering a meal to visitors. A few of the older houses survive. In a street called 'The Loanie' a plaque on a cottage commemorates the signing there by Charles II of the Solemn League and Covenant. Nearby is a house called Stein House, still bearing the name of its builder, the local agent for the Abernethy estate, which sent so much timber to Garmouth. A gentle climb past an old school takes you to the Browlands Standing Stones, from which there are pleasant views all around, notably over Kingston and the estuary of the Spey. Once a year the ladies of the town revive an ancient fair, 'Maggie Fair'.

Kingston is on the seafront just half a mile north of Garmouth. The royal visit was not the reason for Kingston's name: it received it rather because it was founded in 1784 by two timber merchants from York and Kingston-on-Hull, Messrs Ralph Dodsworth and William Osborne – the Glenmore Company. Their plan was to export south the vast resources of the Strathspey pine forests and to start shipbuilding at the mouth of the Spey. They were by no means the first, but the scale of their operations transformed the village on the shore. These operations may be described summarily as the making of dams in Glenmore to create artificial floods to permit logs cut in the forest to be floated down the Spey to Kingston for processing and shipment elsewhere by sea. The company appreciated that they would enjoy greater added value if they used part of the timber to build ships at Kingston. Osborne for this purpose brought from Hull a skilled shipwright, Thomas Hustwick, and in no time at all – by the end of 1785 – a brig of 110 tons, appropriately called the Glenmore, was put to sea. By 1791, apart from small boats, some 19 vessels of a total tonnage exceeding 3500 tons had emerged from their yard. An especially old house is prominent in Kingston, Dunfermline House, formerly called Redcorff House. It was used for a variety of purposes in the past, including accommodation for the staff of the Glenmore Company.

The ample supplies of wood tempted others to follow the Glenmore Company, and soon there were three or four other yards. Longmuir, writing in 1860, describes seeing at Kingston 'the sawmills, the numerous piles of wood, and not fewer than six vessels on the stocks...and a great many vessels have been built here of native timber, and some of them no inconsiderable size.' Jim Skelton, in his book *Speybuilt ... a Forgotten Industry* (Garmouth, 1994), lists many of these and suggests that over 500 with a total tonnage of 83,000 were produced. For a long time Speymouth was regarded as the natural shipping centre for the upper reaches of Speyside. In one year alone 257 vessels entered Speymouth, many of them with local owners and captains, taking in coal and a huge variety of goods and leaving with timber, grain and other agricultural produce. This situation was not to last into the 1880s, partly because of the coming of the railways and partly because the coastal trade was increasingly taken over by steamships, often made of iron, and too large to enter the mouth of the Spey. The ancillary workers lost their jobs and the whole district was dealt a heavy blow. The whirr of the sawmills, the hammering of the shipwrights and all the other sights and sounds of busy shipbuilding yards were no longer to be heard.

SPEYSIDE 'FLOATERS': It may be asked how this shipbuilding and shipping business came to what was certainly the sleepy old village of Garmouth. Although Jim Skelton (p18) records earlier contracts dating from 1630 and 1718, its more recent history may be said to begin with the visit to Speyside of Dodsworth and Osbome, who in 1784 leased from the Duke of Gordon for £26,000 the right to take timber for a period of 26 years from the Duke's extensive forest of Glenmore.

Salmon coble in an ice house

Prior to this time two main methods of sending the timber down the river had been adopted. One was that of 'free-floating' in which logs – often in thousands – were thrown into the river, usually when there was some flooding, natural or artificial, and were escorted down the river by 'floaters' who had the task of freeing any jammed logs. Fifty or more men descended on either side of the river armed with long poles which they used to free any logs stuck on either bank of the river. Men were even stationed at the mouth of the river to prevent logs rushing out to sea, but some logs were inevitably lost. This method, however, presented dangers to bridges – especially when under construction – and an Act of 10th July 1813 entitled procurators fiscal throughout Scotland to recover damages caused by the practice of floating timber.

The other method was to send the logs down river in roughly constructed rafts. Initially the rafts were small, insecurely held together, and guided down the river by men in 'currachs' – defined in 1781 by no less than the House of Lords as 'a small basket of wicker work covered on the outside with an oxhide'.

When, however, the York Buildings Company leased the Strathspey forests in 1728, Aaron Hill had suggested the use of large rafts of 20 to 30 trees. 'In the ends of each tree a hole was bored, and in each a "birch loop" was inserted and fastened with a pin driven in. Through the line of loops at the front and back of the raft a strong rope was run by which the logs were held together without injury to them' (Hamilton Dunnett, *Invera'an: A Speyside Parish*, p146). They were guided generally by two men with large oars, who would steer them round obstructions and deliver them to Garmouth or to sawmills higher up the river.

This second method was followed by Messrs Dodsworth and Osbome when implementing their contract of 1784. They employed gangs of foresters to cut down the timber, to trim it, to cut some of it into various sizes of logs, and to lead it down to the Spey. There, specialist teams of 'floaters' took over and conducted the rafts down to the mouth of the Spey. The contract came to an end in 1806, but the Napoleonic Wars created an immense demand for timber, and other landowners were not slow to supply it. The timber was exported from Garmouth or used in the burgeoning shipbuilding yards of Kingston.

A vivid description of the lives of the floaters is given by Elizabeth Grant of Rothiemurchus (*Memoirs of a Highland Lady,* first published in 1898 – the references are to the edition by Andrew Tod of 1992, pp218–221). A description of the 'Floaters' Ball', the great event of the Christmas period in Rothiemurchus, prompted her to write of the day-to-day life of the foresters and floaters. In the autumn and early winter the foresters felled the trees and lopped the branches, until a deep fall of snow put a stop to this work. The logs were then dragged by little horses to the nearest running water and left there in quantity until the time came for the sluice gates to be opened in small dams higher up the burns. The logs were pushed into the stream and, in the earlier period, picked up at small sawmills lower down these streams. The sawyers sawed the logs, cutting off the bark and might also saw the wood into deals. The logs and deals were then moved to the Spey to be sent down river.

This system was found to be uneconomic and larger sawmills were established at or near the banks of the Spey. This in turn put greater emphasis on the need to manage the flooding, and larger dams and embankments were created higher up the streams, including those at Loch Einich and Loch Morlich. Elizabeth Grant gives a graphic picture of the animation at the point where the logs were rolled into the stream. This was the task of some of the men; the younger and more nimble were those who directed the logs into the current, running downstream with them along the rocks and banks to remove obstructions using their long poles with a clip or sharp hook. Mrs Grant went on to say:

> *'There was something peculiarly graceful in the action of throwing forth the stout yet yielding clip, an exciting satisfaction as the sharp hook found the obstreperous log… The shouts, the gaelick exclamations, and above all the roar of the water, made the whole scene one of the most inspiriting that either Spectators or Actors could be engaged in.'*

Once on the Spey, the Spey floaters took charge of the logs. Mrs Grant continues:

> *'The Spey floaters lived mostly near Ballindalloch, a certain number of families by whom the calling had been followed for ages, to whom the wild river, all its holes and shoals and rocks and shiftings, were as well known as if its bed had been dry. They came up in the season, at the first hint of a speat, as a rise in the water was called. A large bothie was built for them at the mouth of the Druie, in a fashion that suited themselves; a fire in a stone hearth in the middle of the floor, a hole in the very centre of the roof just over it where some of the smoke got out, heather spread on the ground, and there, after their hard day's work, they lay down for the night, in their wet*

clothes – for they had been perhaps for hours in the river – each man's feet to the fire, each man's plaid round his chest, a circle of weary bodies half stupefied by whiskey, enveloped in a cloud of steam and smoke, yet sleeping soundly till the morning. They were a healthy race, suffering little but in their old age from rheumatism. They made their own large rafts themselves, seldom taking any help from our woodmen, yet often giving it if there were an over quantity of timber in the runs.'

In the course of the run down the Spey there were two places that caused particular problems for the floaters. One, in the Spey near Arndilly House, was a submerged rock which was eventually removed by explosives (see Chapter 4). The other was the sharp bend in the River Spey near Knockando, quite close to the meeting point of the Allt Earder Burn with the river (see Chapter 7). The floating of logs down the Spey came to an end with the coming of the railway to Strathspey. That, in the eyes of the Minister of Invera'an, was small compensation for the loss of the sight of the trees of Rothiemurchus rushing down the racing waters of the River Spey. It also soon spelt the end of the major source of employment in Speymouth. Once the wood reached Speymouth some of it was used in the sawmills established there by Messrs Dodsworth and Osborne, cut into deals and planks. One of them was a windmill and operated up to 40 saws and the other a watermill, operating some 36 saws. Some of the wood was sold locally, but the bulk of it was sent by sea to ports around Scotland and, with their own connections, Dodsworth and Osborne sent a lot, in their own boats, to Hull and even to the Royal Dockyards at Deptford and Woolwich. Indeed, they were largely responsible for initiating the practice of shipbuilding in Speymouth, and built ships both to order and on their own account, using the latter chiefly in the Baltic trade.

CHAPTER 4

GARMOUTH TO FOCHABERS

Starting point:	**Where track leaves official route for Garmouth Viaduct**
Distance:	**4.4 miles/7.1km**
Height gained:	**100ft/30m**
Time required:	**2 hours**
Car parking:	**Fochabers village square and elsewhere**
Facilities:	**Shops, hotels, cafes and toilets at Fochabers**
Transport:	**Buses to Elgin, Keith and Aberdeen**

SUMMARY OF ROUTE

Retracing your steps to the point where you were directed to Garmouth, you turn to the right (SWS) and move along pleasant tracks southwards not far from the course of the river. The sounds of the birds wheeling over the path and the river will be heard. From time to time the river comes into view and anglers can be seen patiently casting for salmon from its banks or from cobles in the water. In spring the gorse and broom seem to line the route. They are followed by primroses, catchflies, early purple orchid, wild irises and fireweed. A little before Fochabers the route joins the Spey Bay–Fochabers road for about a quarter of a mile until it enters Bellie Wood and soon nears two bridges across the river. The first is a concrete creation of more utility than elegance and the second an old bridge, clearly constructed at different times. The Way, now close to the river, passes under both bridges. After passing the old bridge the route (SWS) then follows a floodbank (made at the time of construction of the old bridge) and is then signposted to the south-west of Fochabers (see Chapter 4).

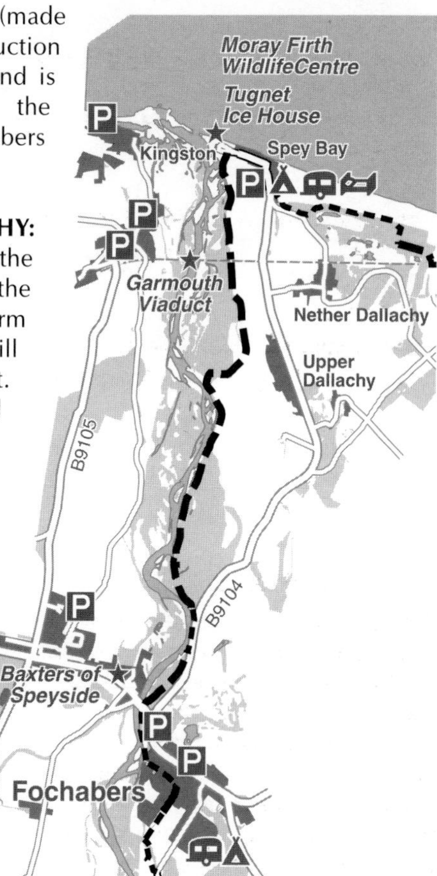

NETHER DALLACHY: After returning over the Spey Viaduct to the Speyside Way, the farm of Nether Dallachy will be seen to the east. When it was a typical quiet, hard-working Banffshire farm it was commemorated by a North East poet, J M Caie:

Way doon in Nether Dallachy
There's neither watch nor knock,
There's denner time and supper time
And aye, Yoke! Yoke!

The Dallachy memorial

This quiet was harshly disturbed during the Second World War. From 1943 onwards an RAF strike wing was stationed at Dallachy. It flew twin-engined Beaufighters carrying rockets. Their mission was to attack German U-boats and other shipping in the North Sea, including ships carrying iron ore from Norwegian ports to Germany. While they inflicted heavy losses on the enemy, they did not all survive unscathed. On one day, 7th February 1945, nine Beaufighters from Dallachy and one escorting Mustang were lost: a memorial erected just off the Speyside Way near the hamlet of Bogmoor records these events. Dallachy was once home to the Highland Gliding Club, whose members took advantage of the normally good weather in this part of the country and the useful thermals.

OLD FOCHABERS BRIDGE: Before the old bridge was built there was merely an inadequate ferry across the Spey, a little to the north, called Boat of Bog. Though there was more than one ferryboat there were constant complaints about the service, and eventually the Duchess of Gordon spearheaded an appeal for funds for a bridge. When finance became available c1802, Telford was commissioned to build it. Although the bridge was to have four arches, the work was completed as soon as 1804. A watercolour of the original bridge by James Giles is on view in Brodie Castle.

When the flood of 1829 reached the bridge it held for a little and some young men ventured on to it to view the scene. Suddenly they heard a cracking noise above the roar of the waters. The roadway for a moment seemed to hold good but, in the words of one of them, *'...ere I had time to cry out, it was falling in a thousand pieces... I sprang sideways... and leaped from fragment to fragment of the falling roadway as if I had been flying'*. This lad escaped, but the lame young son of the tollkeeper was less quick and was drowned. Efforts were made to replace as soon as possible the two fallen arches with a wooden arch of 185ft/56m. This stood until 1859 but, being threatened with dry rot, was replaced by the present cast-iron arch. So the old bridge, as repaired, still stands but, being unsuitable for modern loads, these are now carried by the concrete bridge opened in 1972.

It is worth crossing the old bridge to enjoy the views south to Ben Aigan and Ben Rinnes. A few minutes should be taken to glance at the old Toll House at the west end of the bridge. The Toll House has been sympathetically extended to the north. Directly opposite stand the premises of Baxters of Speyside, a family firm which, starting as a small concern in Fochabers, has become known worldwide for its soups, jams and other produce. Visitors are welcome and come in large numbers to look round the factory and to sample its products in the excellent visitor centre. The temptation to do so is resisted only by persons impervious to the pleasure of eating freshly made pancakes with strawberry jam. Baxters are not, perhaps, in the best of locations from a distribution standpoint; but their striking successes at home and abroad illustrate what can be done by a team dedicated to quality and innovation.

Old Spey Bridge at Fochabers

FOCHABERS: The walker or cyclist will find, on returning to the east side of the Spey, that the Speyside Way strictly goes along the west side of the town of Fochabers. It seems better, however, to get the feel of the place by wandering through it. The grandiose entrance to Gordon Castle is seen shortly to the east. It has high, curving walls on either side, which meet in a high, arched main gate flanked by two porters' lodges. From there a carriageway sweeps on for some half a mile before reaching what remains of the formerly spectacular castle. The original tower of six storeys, almost 90ft/27m in height, is preserved and a substantial part of the east wing. But this gives no more than a hint of the princely magnificence of the castle as it stood in the 1930s before the death of the last Duke of Richmond and Gordon. The castle had a frontage of 568ft/173m and looked onto attractively laid out gardens tended by an army of gardeners.

The village and toll cross of old Fochabers were situated quite close to old Gordon Castle. When, however, in 1776 the fourth Duke decided to rebuild the castle, he chose for the village – which had been adjacent to the castle – a site nearer the Spey and commissioned his own architect, John Baxter, to plan the village. Baxter did so on a grid system with the principal subordinate streets parallel to the main road. To many, Fochabers has epitomised the Scottish country village, but no less a person than Lord Cockburn – who was no admirer of the Dukes or the ostentation of their castle – remarked:

> *'The inn here is excellent. And if the village had been less regular, and less obviously withdrawn in its structure from the will of the people, it would have been better. But the truth is that during the lives of the two last dukes – a period probably of sixty years – it was neither meant nor used as a village for villagers, but as a kennel for the retired laqueys and ladies'-maids of the castle and for the natural children and pensioned mistresses of the noble family…'* (*Circuit Journeys*, Edinburgh, 1888, p154).

But Lord Cockburn may have been letting his Whig political opinions cloud his appreciation of the architecture of (new) Fochabers.

Returning to the High Street you will soon see on the left the inn which Cockburn praised, the Gordon Arms (c1810), a line of old shops on either side of the road, and then the village square. On its right-hand side is the (new) Bellie Kirk. It is a building of more than local architectural importance, flanked on either side by fine two-storeyed houses. The square had a pleasant symmetry, but was not enhanced by the centrally situated bus station and lavatories. In a spirit of architectural correctness the latter were recently removed, but the nearest alternative is some distance away beside the playing fields on the road which becomes the Ordiequish road. There are two other modestly attractive churches, the Episcopal Chapel and the RC Church. The former seems unusual: the services are held on the first floor rather than the ground floor and it is embellished with fine stained-glass windows. The RC Church is tucked away in South Street, a street which seems to encapsulate the discreet charms of Fochabers.

Moving up the High Street, the Fochabers Folk Museum is to be seen on the left, a converted church whose stained-glass windows and vaulted roof are no less interesting than the exhibits. Higher up, on the right, is the former 'Milne's Institution' – now a primary school – which Moray owes to the munificent benefaction of one of her sons who had emigrated to America and made a fortune there. We are told that he left the service of the Duke of Gordon rather than have his hair cut as required. At the end of the High Street, where the Keith–Huntly road diverges to the right, Christie's Nurseries, founded in 1820, has a garden centre and cafe. To return from here to the Speyside Way, turn about to the north and take the first road on the left which, after passing the police station and playing fields (with toilets), leads on to the Ordiequish road, where the Speyside Way is signposted.

WINDING WALKS: If you plan to spend a little more time in Fochabers, a visit to the local 'Winding Walks' is suggested. About half a mile east of Christie's Nurseries a Forestry Commission car park marks the starting point of these walks. They were planned over a century ago by the then Duke of Gordon who planted a gully in Whiteash Hill with a variety of ornamental trees and shrubs. Many of these survive. Near the highest point of these walks is a striking memorial erected in 1887 to Frances Harriet, Duchess of Richmond. Nearby is Whiteash Hill Monument Viewpoint, giving a bird's-eye view of the mouth of the Spey, and the inner Moray Firth.

CHAPTER 5

FOCHABERS TO CRAIGELLACHIE

Starting point:	**At NJ 342594, south of Old Fochabers Bridge**
Distance:	**12.5 miles/20.1km**
Height gained:	**In all, some 1000ft/300m**
Time required:	**6–7 hours**
Car parking:	**Limited parking near Old Fochabers Bridge and elsewhere in Fochabers. Limited parking at Boat O'Brig**
Facilities:	**Shops, hotels, B&Bs and cafes in Fochabers. There are subsequently no facilities until Craigellachie.**

Summary of route

The next section of the Speyside Way follows the east bank of the river from Fochabers to Boat o'Brig and then to Craigellachie. It skirts Fochabers on its south-west side beside the Spey until it meets the Burn of Fochabers, which it follows on the true right-hand side until it meets (SWS) a road passing Fochabers High School. It turns to the right along this road and keeps straight on, passing a new housing development on the right until it meets another burn, the Burn of Ordiequish, which it soon crosses and follows on its south side until it meets the Ordiequish road. Here SWS point to the right and the road gently rises until a Forest Enterprise sign invites visitors to Slorach's Wood. A few yards further on there is a makeshift car park on the right. This is the point of entry to a feature of Alltdearg, a geological site of special scientific interest (SSSI), referred to below. After this point the road descends steeply down to the Alltdearg Burn, crosses it and then climbs equally steeply upwards. After this, it is a pleasant stroll along the road above the Craigs of Cuildell, past Craiglug, Whitehillock and Cairnty before descending steeply through woodlands above Delfur Lodge until Boat o'Brig is reached. There is a small car park here.

There are two bridges at Boat o'Brig. The northern is a railway bridge carrying the Keith–Elgin railway over the Spey and the southern is a road bridge. An SWS here directs the visitor to take a path upwards to the left of a former toll house at the east end of the road bridge. When a farm track is reached another SWS indicates that the Way goes south to

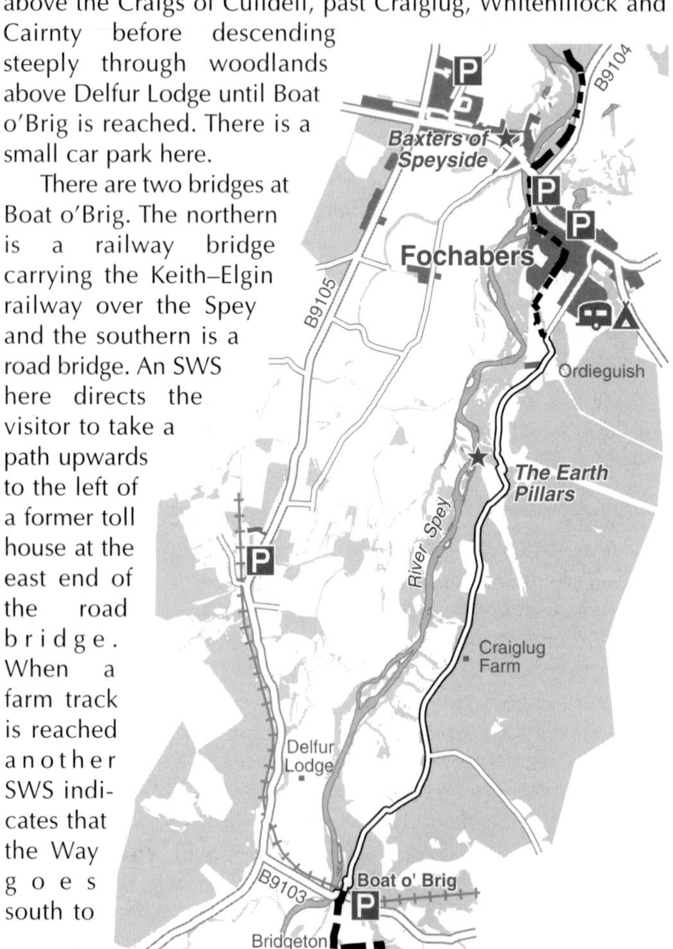

Bridgeton Farm, now apparently derelict. Passing it, the route swings eastwards past a cottage on the left until a SWS indicates that the route goes south. Soon it passes two gates and a nearby shooting range and then travels south-west beside fencing, a route giving pleasant views to the north. Shortly, the route swings east of south (SWS) up a steepish path to the left of the Allt Daley Burn, here forming quite a canyon. Before long a broad forestry path is met (SWS) which is followed to tables and benches, allowing a pleasant break. The route – adequately signposted – now starts its long descent towards Arndilly House. When approaching this house from the north, pine trees give way to others, with tall beech trees lining the road. As the scene becomes more open, there are fine views southwards towards Ben Rinnes and up the River Spey. Above and to the left of the road there are occasional glimpses of Ben Aigan. This hill is some 1500ft/450m high and, because of its northerly position, affords wide-ranging views, not only of Ben Rinnes, the Spey and the Laich of Moray, but – on a clear day – the Cannich hills and those of Ross and Cromarty. It is usually climbed from a Forest Enterprise car park adjacent to the estate of Auchlunkart.

From Arndilly there is pleasant walking though mixed woods to the Fiddichside Inn, near the bridge carrying the A95 over the Fiddich. Across the bridge lies Fiddichside Park, the site of the old Craigellachie Railway Station and the offices of the Speyside Way Ranger Service (tel. 01340 881266). Camping may be permitted here, and there is an adjacent car park.

ALLTDEARG: At the lay-by here (not signposted) a well-constructed path leads to one of the Fochabers Earth Pillars, a geological SSSI, well worth visiting. The ground here is a species of red sandstone conglomerate, and large capstones have protected some of it from erosion, giving the effect of strange giants surveying the scene. Similar capstones could be seen from the 'drumlins' of the A96 before it was improved and when

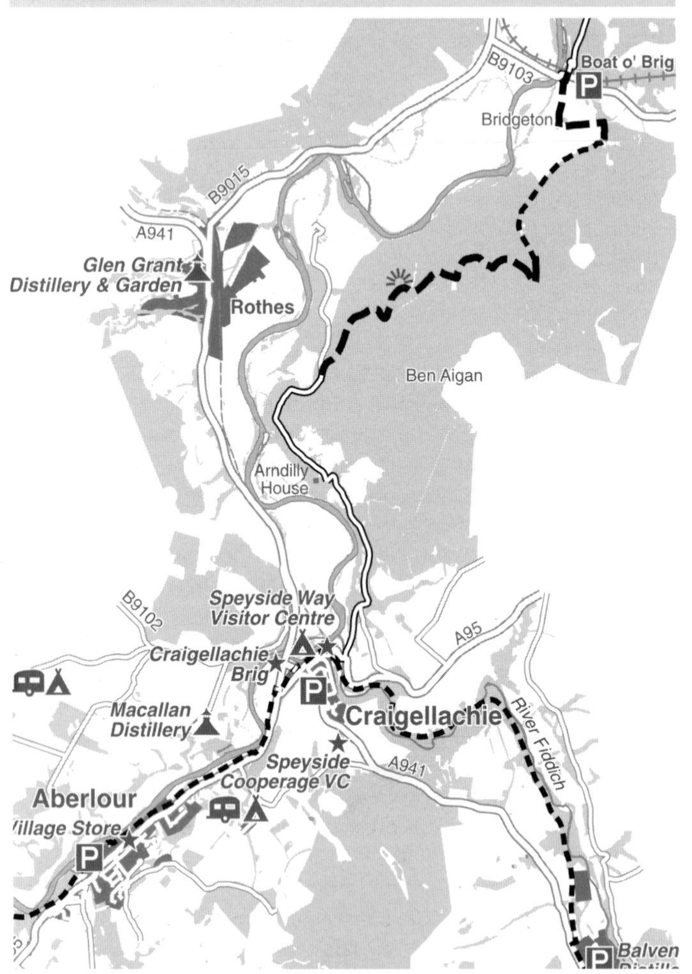

the burn of Fochabers was less heavily wooded. It can hardly be claimed that these pillars are as spectacular as those which world travellers may have seen but they did greatly excite A E

Knox who, in his *Autumns on the Spey* (1872), was for once diverted from his favourite sport of salmon fishing. After explaining how the earth pillars arose, he adds:

> *'The professed geologist, indeed, can discover many other places in this district, and on the banks of the Spey itself, calculated to illustrate these interesting facts, but the lover of nature will not appreciate scientific truth the less from its being associated with such novel and quaint scenery as is exhibited in the gorge of the Alt Degree and its tributary ravines'* (p132).

BOAT O'BRIG: The name is a reminder that there was a wooden bridge here in medieval times, maintained, with an adjacent hospice dedicated to St Nicholas, from the produce of lands gifted for this purpose in 1232. The bridge fell down in post-medieval times but a ferryboat was established here to carry people across the Spey. Following the floods of 1829 a suspension bridge was erected to carry both pedestrian and road traffic. It was of a not uncommon design at that period, with a single tower at either side pierced by an archway to allow traffic to cross. It remained in service until replaced in 1954 by the present, more utilitarian structure. Downstream of this bridge is a railway viaduct, constructed c1856, to carry the line from Keith to Elgin. It is essentially an iron-girder structure 230ft/70m in length, with six side arches on the west side to allow the passage of flood waters.

While at Boat o'Brig a diversion could be made to see the Auchroisk Distillery, less than 1.4 miles/2km down the Keith road. It is worth a visit since, rebuilt in 1973, it is one of the most elegant of Speyside distilleries. There is no tradtional pagoda vent since the malted barley is now bought in, but its jagged roof-line and functional simplicity are attractive.

ARNDILLY HOUSE: The route passes close to Arndilly House, built c1750 on the site of the old church of Ardentoll. It

Arndilly House

remained for a century as a rather plain, square building but was rebuilt in a more romantic style by the Elgin architect, Thomas Mackenzie. The house has a fine entrance porch, supported by four massive pillars. There are the compulsory square keep and the inevitable sprinkling of smaller towers. There is also a fine conservatory with terraces below leading down to the Spey. A relic of the past is built into a wall of the house about 10m beyond the front entrance. This is a Pictish stone – perhaps upside down – with a 'mirror case' and 'Z-rod', the latter ornamented at its ends. Though a little cut down it is a splendid example of stone-carving skills. Permission to view it should be sought at the house.

Near Arndilly, as Elizabeth Grant tells us,

> *'There was a sunken rock [in the Spey] sometimes difficult to pass; this formed a means of livelihood to several families living on the spot. It was their privilege to provide ropes, and arms to*

pull the ropes! and so help the floats through a rapid current running in high floods between this sunken rock and the shore. The dole they got was small, yet there were hardly more outcry in Sutherland when the Duke wanted his starving cottars to leave their turf huts on the moors to live in comfortable stone and lime houses by the sea, than my father met when some years after this he got leave to remove this obstacle by blasting' (*Memoirs of a Highland Lady*, p229).

CHAPTER 6

THE DUFFTOWN SPUR

Starting point:	**Speyside Way Visitor Centre at Craigellachie**
Distance:	**4 miles/6.4km**
Height gained:	**200ft/60m**
Time required:	**2.5 hours**
Car parking:	**Near the visitor centre and in Dufftown**
Facilities:	**In Dufftown, an information centre and various hotels, restaurants, B&Bs, shops, a post office and toilets**
Transport:	**There is an intermittent bus service to and fro between Aberlour, Craigellachie and Dufftown.**

SUMMARY OF ROUTE

A 'spur' of the Speyside Way normally takes the walker or cyclist from Craigellachie to Dufftown along the former track of the railway between those places. At the time of writing, however, a landslip caused by heavy rain has temporarily – it is hoped – caused the route to be closed. When the route is available it is accessible from the Ranger Services Office. Cross under the A95 to the small car park west of it and SWS signs may be followed to the former railway viaduct across the lower Fiddich. The route follows its sparkling waters for about a mile up a quite narrow gorge. Though less than 1000ft/300m across, it is some 150–250ft/50–80m deep. The route gradually rises through lovely woods on the true right bank of the Fiddich.

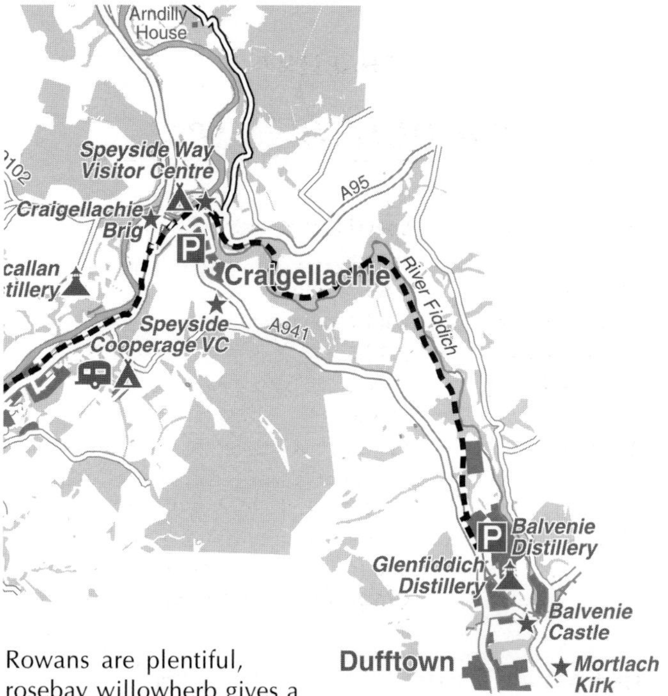

Rowans are plentiful, rosebay willowherb gives a dash of colour and there are lots of wild roses and smaller plants. After a mile the Fiddich is crossed by Newton Bridge which offers dramatic views of the river and its gorge. The route still rises gradually but the views open out, and there are fields on the right with Little Conval above them. Soon Convalmore Distillery comes into view and the Speyside Way exits on the A941 road (SWS) to Dufftown. Shortly the old goods station on the Keith line and the far-famed Glenfiddich Distillery are passed, and Dufftown itself is entered. Dufftown has every facility for the tourist: an information office, hotels, B&Bs, restaurants, cafes, chip shops, pubs, a golf course and other sporting facilities.

DUFFTOWN: The town claims to be considered the whisky capital of Scotland. What other town earns as much foreign exchange per head of population? It is the site of the Glenfiddich Distillery (1887) but also of Mortlach (1823), Balvenie (1892), Convalmore (1894) (now closed), Pittyvaich (1975) (now closed) and Kininvie (1992).

But Dufftown has other claims for notice in the secular and religious history of Scotland. The town was created by the Earl of Fife after the Napoleonic Wars, primarily to create jobs. Its

Dufftown clock tower

centrepiece is the clock tower (c1839) which was designed to house the Burgh Chambers and the local gaol. It now houses an admirable tourist information office. The clock came from Banff and the story goes that this was the clock that was advanced an hour, so preventing receipt by the authorities of a pardon for James McPherson, the freebooting fiddler. The austerity of Fife Street, descending from the Clock Tower, is diminished by a series of shops and restaurants. The street leads down to Balvenie Castle, the Glenfiddich Distillery and, eventually, the road to Craigellachie. East from the Clock Tower is Church Street. To the west you may take the Tomintoul road which, in little more than a couple of miles, leads to a popular starting-point for Ben Rinnes (see below).

MORTLACH: By turning sharp right near the foot of Church Street, Mortlach Parish Church may be visited. Its congregation played an important part in the annals of the Disruption, when the Free Church for doctrinal reasons broke away from the Church of Scotland. Though the older part of the church dates back to the 13th century, the church as extended in the 19th century is rather plain. Within it is the wall tomb of a knight in armour – possibly Alexander Leslie of Kininvie – dating from the early 16th century. There is also a stone carrying a beautifully incised 'Pictish elephant' and a strange non-representational ogee-like shape. Beneath the church in the lower churchyard stands a largish stone – apparently a natural pillar – which carries on one side a cross with two fish monsters with animal heads above and a four-legged creature below and on the other side representations (visible only with the eyes of faith) of a bird, a serpent, a bull's head and a mounted man with accompanying dog. Sadly, if the stone conveys a message it is, and is likely to remain, unclear. The cemetery overlooks the Dullan Water, up which there is an attractive walk (signposted) to the Giant's Chair and thence back to Mortlach, passing en route Pittyvaich and Mortlach distilleries.

GLENFIDDICH DISTILLERY AND SPEYSIDE COOPERAGE: Glenfiddich Distillery lies near Balvenie Castle to the north of the town and welcomes visitors. It no longer malts its own barley but is otherwise quite typical of the older style of Speyside malt distillery. It still has its own bottling plant. The Dufftown distilleries have attracted ancillary industries, including the interesting 'Speyside Cooperage', formerly situated within the town but now in more ample premises to the west of the Dufftown–Craigellachie road. It makes or repairs some 100,000 casks a year and has a visitor centre with an excellent display (tel: 01340 871108). It explains the history of the cooper's craft and from its viewing gallery the visitor can see the coopers at work.

BALVENIE CASTLE: Dufftown boasts the castle of Balvenie, grey, grim and large. It was a stronghold of the Comyns, visited by Edward I in 1304 and Mary, Queen of Scots, in 1562. After the Comyns it belonged to the Black Douglases and the Stewart Earls of Atholl. As we see it today there is a moat along two sides, the other two moats having been obliterated in the later 16th century, when the castle was transposed into something approaching a stately mansion. Its imposing Renaissance facade has three storeys and a mansarded roof. The curtain walls enclose an impressive courtyard with a narrow entrance, a small guardroom and all the offices expected in contemporary castles: a bakehouse, brewhouse, kitchens and cellars. A feature is the two-leaved iron yett or gate. When one thinks of the relative poverty of its location, the castle seems an expensive luxury; but then, in the past, it was of considerable military importance, commanding the confluence of glens Rinnes and Fiddich, the routes to the Royal Castles of Rothes, Elgin and Cullen and, with Auchindoun, the route over the Cabrach to Deeside.

BEN RINNES: The summit of Ben Rinnes (2760ft/840m) is only some 6 miles/10km from Dufftown and makes a popular and agreeable excursion. It is most easily climbed from the B9009 – the Tomintoul road – where a country road branches off to the Glack Harnes, a narrow glen between Ben Rinnes and Meikle Conval. About a mile up this road is a small car park with a signpost pointing to a route up the Ben. The lower part of the track past Roy's Hill has been improved thanks to the 'Friends of Ben Rinnes', but the part close to the summit, the Scurran of Lochterlandach, has been badly eroded and widened by the numbers climbing the hill. It is deservedly popular, since the views in good weather from the top over the Laich of Moray and the whole Moray Firth are superlative. On a clear day they extend, we are told, as far as the Cannich hills. On a summer's day there are often many locals, even parents carrying babies or walking with extremely independent youngsters. But beware: in winter the route is unusually exposed and you may be lashed by snow and icy winds as fierce as any to be encountered in the Cairngorms. The Scurran is one of three tors reminiscent of those on Ben Avon or Beinn Mheadoin. Ben Rinnes, like the Cairngorms, is a granite hill and shows the same signs of tabular weathering. The descent is a joy, with its views of the Convals and other nearby hills.

KEITH AND DUFFTOWN RAILWAY: This railway, in reality part of the GNSR, reached Dufftown as early as 1861. It was soon, as the Strathspey Railway, to join Craigellachie with Boat of Garten. Passenger traffic on this line ceased in October 1963 and the line was finally closed by British Railways three years later. Recently restored by the Keith and Dufftown Railway Association (tel. 01340 821181), in the summer months this heritage railway is reopened, running through picturesque scenery to Loch Park, Drummuir Castle and to Keith.

CHAPTER 7

CRAIGELLACHIE TO KNOCKANDO

Starting point:	**Speyside Way Visitor Centre**
Distance:	**6.4 miles/10.4km**
Height gained:	**200ft/60m**
Time required:	**With visit to Aberlour, 3.5 hours**
Car parking:	**At visitor centre, in Aberlour, at Carron and at Knockandu**
Facilities:	**Large variety at Aberlour. Limited at Knockandu village, a mile from Knockandu Station**
Transport:	**Limited service to Aberlour and Dufftown**

SUMMARY OF ROUTE

From Craigellachie southwards the Speyside Way follows the former track of the Speyside Railway to Aberlour and eventually to Ballindalloch. Leaving Fiddich Park towards the south it passes under a road bridge and swings sharply to the left to follow the course of the Spey. The track passes under the Craigellachie by-pass and through a small cutting, then goes via a tunnel through the rock called Taminurie, or 'Fairies' Crag'. The tunnel was the only one on that railway. The track soon crosses an iron girder bridge before going past a steep cutting overhanging it and the River Spey. On its upper side the route is protected by a massive retaining wall some 50ft/15m or more in height. These relics of the railway line give a clear impression of the difficulties faced by its constructors. This part of the route is decorated by a profusion of flowers, not all wild. There are wild roses, wood anemones, blaeberries and many others. The cutting is soon left, but the track as it moves towards Aberlour remains close to the Spey. In this short stretch railway enthusiasts will notice many artefacts associated with the former railway. The old railway station at Aberlour has been converted into a simple wayside cafe, looked after by local ladies. It is worth looking around the town.

From the site of the old station in Aberlour the Speyside Way follows the south bank of the Spey to Carron. A pedestrian suspension bridge crossing the river is soon seen to the right, but is not crossed. Head directly ahead to a Speyside Way noticeboard and map. Obliquely to the left (SWS) the former track of the Speyside Railway is followed, first through a cutting for some 200–300m and then through woods until the secondary road to Carron is met. On the right-hand side are the grounds of Carron House. Near here is the site of the former siding at Daluaine Halt from which a track, closed in 1971, led to Daluaine Distillery. The road to Carron soon crosses the Spey (SWS) by a former dual rail/road bridge which leads the walker – and the motorist – to the village of Carron. The bridge (see below) is interesting in its own right. The Speyside Way carries on to the sites of the former Carron Railway Station and of the former, patriotically named, Imperial Distillery, established in 1897 when Queen Victoria had her Diamond Jubilee. But only a century later the distillery was closed and, without it, the village seems likely to die. From here, the Speyside Way continues along the track of the old railway, usually close to the river though at one bend, where there is a fertile haugh, llamas may be seen grazing peacefully. In autumn there are the vivid colours of rowanberries and of leaves about to fall. This is an attractive route at most times of the year, and must have given pleasure to the rail passengers. Soon the Way reaches Knockandu Distillery with its pagoda-like vent, the former site of Knockando Station and, shortly after it, Tamdhu Distillery.

CRAIGELLACHIE: The village of Craigellachie developed because it was chosen as a junction connecting the railway lines from Keith and Elgin to the Speyside line. All three were effectively part of the GNSR network. It also had the advantage of being for some time close to the most northerly bridge over the Spey. With the railways had come hotels, other accommodation, a post office and a few shops, and these continue to offer tourists hospitality and services. The village remains, too, a useful centre for salmon fishers on the Spey. The Speyside Railway closed in 1868, but Craigellachie remains an attractive tourist centre. There are several nearby malt distilleries but, apart from the Macallan Distillery, none is open to the public.

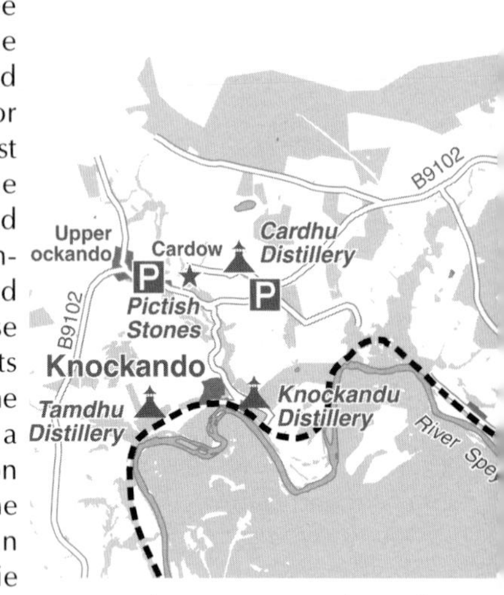

'CRAIGELLACHIE BRIG': The most interesting feature, however, of the village is the old Spey Bridge. This was designed, like the Fochabers Bridge, by Telford and erected under the supervision of his assistant, John Simpson. It took 10 months to build and was opened in October 1814. Telford had originally planned to have lower abutments, but Simpson listened to local advice and placed them 12ft/3.5m above the normal water level. This enabled the bridge to withstand the extraordinary floods of 1829 and to survive today as a thing of simplicity and unusual beauty. The bridge is even commemorated in a Highland dance, the Strathspey 'Craigellachie Brig'. It is not easy to appreciate today what a feat of engineering and planning the work represented. The cast-iron sections for the bridge were made at Plas

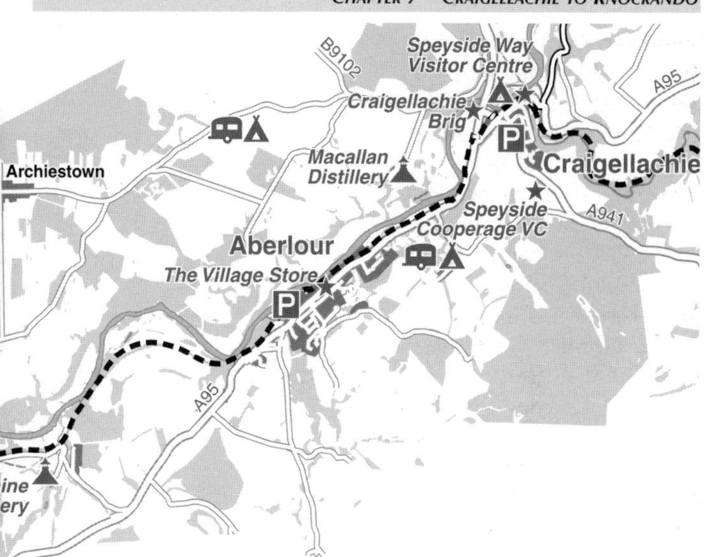

Kynaston, Denbighshire, Wales, and taken by barge to the sea where they were transported by ship to Kingston. The sections were then loaded upon wagons and taken up Strathspey on its then most indifferent roads to Craigellachie, where the sections were erected on prepared foundations to form the arch whose elegance still attracts attention.

ABERLOUR: This village, like several others on the Way, was a planned village. Charles Grant of Wester Elchies founded it in 1812, advertising for incomers and being generous with the size of his feus. Some aspects of the recent history of the place are illustrated in the 'Village Shop' – perhaps more a lovingly collected museum of domestic articles – on the main street at the north-east corner of the town square. The village today has an air of confidence and prosperity. That is not merely due to the presence of its distilleries but to that of Walkers of Aberlour, bakers, who in 1999 won for the third time the Queen's award for export achievement. The company gives employment, apart from seasonal workers, to some 500 local men and women. Their shortbread and cakes are of national and international renown. To the west of the town are the ruins of St Drostan's Kirk and cemetery. Nearby is an old packhorse bridge over the Aberlour Burn. Some distance up the burn is the Lyne of Ruthrie, a waterfall which was the scene of one of several tragic deaths during the Muckle Spate of 1829.

DAILUAINE DISTILLERY: Alfred Barnard, whose ground-breaking study of *The Whisky Distilleries of the United Kingdom* was published in 1887, declared that the 1851 Dailuaine Distillery 'graced one of the prettiest little glens in Scotland'. He had, of course, been privileged to visit it on 'the perfection of a summer's day... Never was such a soft, bright landscape of luxuriant green, of clustering foliage, and the verdant banks, ferns and grasses. The whole scene is dainty enough for a fairy's palace' (*Whisky Distilleries*, p201). Outside the distillery all was peace and quiet: inside it, however, all was *'life, bustle, and activity, and the establishment a little world of industry in itself... No wonder with these surroundings that the pure spirit emerging from such an Eden should be appreciated by mortals all the world over'*. Today, the surroundings are equally attractive. Though the buildings show their age, the impression the distillery gives is less of life, bustle and activity than of quiet efficiency, producing enormously more whisky with many fewer staff. Not only whisky is produced. Since 1934 Dailuaine, using products from neighbouring distilleries also, has concentrated pot ale, a product of distilling, to a syrup and mixed it with dried draff to produce what are called 'dark grains' – a superior form of cattle feed relatively high in proteins.

CARRON BRIDGE: The road to Carron crosses the Spey by a former dual rail/road bridge which leads the walker – and the motorist – to the village of Carron. The bridge is interesting in

Distilleries below the hills (Chapter 6)

'Craigellachie Brig' (Chapter 7)

Packhorse bridge below Deskie over the Livet (Chapter 9)

Down Conglass Water past Croughly Farm (Chapter 9)

Leaving Knockfrink Wood (Chapter 10)

View from Knockfrink up Speyside (Chapter 10)

Below Cromdale Hills (Chapter 10)

Salmon fishing on the Spey near Grantown (Chapter 10)

Carron Bridge

its own right. Built in 1863, it has three arches, the central one being of cast iron with a span of 150ft/45m, the last of its kind to be built for a railway in Scotland. Cast iron was soon replaced, first by wrought iron and then by steel. It is a bow truss bridge, standing some 40ft/12m above the water: this fact and the two wide side arches of stone show that its designer took full account of the lessons of the Muckle Spate of 1829. The view to the west from the bridge is magnificent. The river is deep and fast flowing and swirls round and over boulders between steep-sided banks of forest. Once over Carron Bridge a diversion may be made along a country track which turns off to the right. Though not part of the Way, visiting it is a pleasant diversion. The road follows the left bank of the Spey to the picturesque Laggan House. The route is bordered by a variety of old trees and carpeted with seasonal flowers. The Spey is never far away, its eddies flashing in the sunlight.

CHAPTER 8

KNOCKANDO TO BALLINDALLOCH

Starting point:	**Former station at Knockandu**
Distance:	**4.3 miles/7km**
Height gained:	**80ft/25m**
Time required:	**2 hours**
Car parking:	**Knockandu Station, Blacksboat and former Ballindalloch Station**
Facilities:	**None**
Transport:	**Enquire locally**

Summary of route

After Knockandu Distillery the Speyside Way soon passes the substantial relics of an old railway station. This was built in 1899 and by 1905 was called Knockando, since it served the adjacent village of that name (see below). The principal building now carries the sign 'Knockandu'. A short distance beyond Knockandu Station the Way crosses the Knockando Burn. It is difficult to imagine this today, but during the spate of 1829 it reached the normal size of the River Spey and destroyed several cottages as well as a meal mill and a carding mill. An old railway viaduct takes you over the stream. Skirting Tamdhu Distillery, the track now passes beneath an impressively large salmon hatchery and then begins to curve round until it moves in a southerly direction. Here a viaduct crosses the Allt Earder Burn (see below) near its meeting point with the Spey.

From this point onwards the railway track has been cut into the edge of a steep hillside sloping down to the river. In spring there are many primroses and other flowers. The Way is now

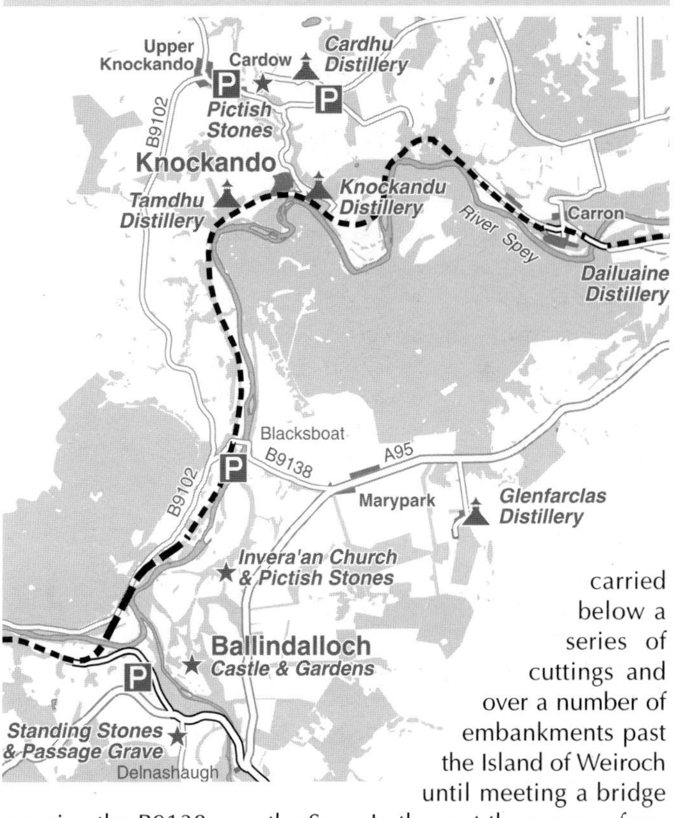

carried below a series of cuttings and over a number of embankments past the Island of Weiroch until meeting a bridge carrying the B9138 over the Spey. In the past there was a ferry here, once called the Boat of Pithaish, and later called Blacksboat, after the name of the brothers who at one time lived at Pithaish. The first bridge was built here in 1908, no doubt to the distress of 'Boatie' Macpherson, ferryman for the preceding 40 years. The Speyside Railway Station here was called 'Blacksboat' and one of its stone buildings survives in good order. There is a Speyside Way noticeboard here, Blacksboat being one of its joining points, and some parking for cars is

Blacksboat Station building

available. The old railway goods shed reminds the visitor of bygone days. The track of the Speyside Way is now close to the river and follows its generally south-west direction. The walking is easy and the most significant feature of the route is the new and elegantly economical bridge over the Allt a Gheallaidh Burn. The valley here opens out considerably and the views to the east are particularly attractive. The west slopes of Ben Rinnes naturally dominate the scene, though the nearer views towards Invera'an Parish Church (see below) and the grounds of Ballindalloch Castle (see below) are largely obscured by trees.

Continuing along the Speyside Way the track soon reaches another viaduct across the Spey, an iron bridge of some 198ft/60m. A metal plate announces that it was the work of 'G. McFarlane, Engineer, Dundee'. No doubt he was proud of his work and the bridge is now a listed building. The rails have been removed and wooden planks and a handrail provided. Crossing the bridge there is on the left the site of an old timber yard used for sending pit props and other timber south during the two world wars. There is here a profusion of wild flowers and garden escapes. The route approaches a house, still marked Ballindalloch in large letters. The house is the former station building and marked until recently the southern end of the Speyside Way. Its route now continues to Aviemore following the main track of the old line. At this point you have three options. The first is to seize the chance of visiting Ballindalloch Castle and/or the Church of Invera'an, both referred to below. The second is to traverse the 'spur' route to Tomintoul which is described in the following chapter. The third, which is by no means incompatible with completing the preceding options, is to press on towards Grantown-on-Spey.

KNOCKANDO: The village of Knockando itself lies a little more than half a mile to the north of the station. Unlike the nearby village of Archieston, which was one of the 'planned' villages of

Cardhu Distillery, Knockando

Speyside, Knockando is quite determinedly unplanned and lies higgledy-piggledy on a shelf of land above the river. It has an interesting kirk dating from 1757, though drastically altered in 1906, notably with a prominent round tower of French style. Just beyond the entrance gates to the churchyard three pictish stones are built into the wall. They are not especially clear, but that nearest to the gate shows a wheel and two crescents and V-rods. The stone next to it is very worn away but there are traces of a serpent, mirror and comb. The third stone retains its own secrets.

It may be, however, that Knockando's main attraction to the visitor will be the Cardhu Distillery, which lies a little above and to the east of the village. Distilling on the site goes back to 1812, though it was not until 1830 that John Cumming took out a licence. Like John Walker and Sons – who purchased the operation in 1893 – the distillery is still going strong. Visits are encouraged and, though the malted barley is now bought in, the methods used are otherwise quite traditional. It produces a pleasant single malt whisky matured for 12 years which, although sold in the gift shop, mostly goes for blending.

ALLT EARDER BURN: Trees now conceal the course of the burn, but in one night in 1829 it cut out a ravine some 80ft/24m deep and at least 150ft/45m wide, carrying thousands of tons of earth and stones into the Spey. Over this ravine the railwaymen had to build a three-spanned bridge, some 50ft/15m in height – a task not made easy by the problem of securing firm foundations for the central arches. It was near this point, too, where the river takes a sharp turn at Tamdhu, that the Spey floaters had their most dangerous task. Here 'the river dashes with such force and rapidity against the cliff, and at right angles to it, that the floats of wood to Garmouth were formerly broken to pieces with the violence of the collision' (Revd Hamilton Dunnett, *Invera'an: A Speyside Parish*, Paisley, 1919, p147). It was necessary to double-man the floats, and here the floaters found help at the farm of Delvargan on the opposite bank. For

Invera'an Church

his pains the tenant apparently was given a tree or log from the float. The problem was so serious that the York Buildings Company is said to have cut out a channel through the land on the Delvargan side (J Murdoch, *Speyside: its Scenery and Antiquities*, Elgin, 1876, p61). At times of flood the scene at the rock of Tamdhu will certainly be dramatic.

INVERA'AN CHURCH: The church of Invera'an is in a choice situation, overlooking the waters of the Spey and the track recently followed. The history of the church was lovingly recorded by the Revd Hamilton Dunnett. He wrote vividly of the lives of the 'floaters' on the Spey and explained that the burning of the 'clavie' was not confined to sea-coast places like Burghead, and often thought of as a druidical fire-ritual to protect the boats. In 1704 an Act of the Kirk Session here forbade 'The custome of going thorow ye cornes wt. clavies' (Dunnett, op. cit., p99). The penalties were severe, even affecting children. He also describes the symbol stones now affixed to the church wall, and refers, among others, to the well-incised large eagle and 'Pictish elephant'.

Ballindalloch Castle

BALLINDALLOCH CASTLE: Ballindalloch Castle and its gardens must certainly be visited. Douglas Simpson writes:

> *'For the perfect picture of an ancient Highland castle, where a noble river, spacious and finely wooded grounds, and a background of forest rising into a crest of wine-dark hills, all combine to set forth a coronet of turrets, steep roofs with crow-stepped gables and picturesque dormer windows ... we may perhaps turn, among all the baronial mansions in our area, to Ballindalloch Castle in Strathspey, in the angle where the Avon meets the Spey'* (W D Simpson, Occasional Papers, Aberdeen University Library, Special Collections).

The castle proclaims itself to have been erected in 1540 and restored in 1850, but over time has attracted many alterations and additions. These are part of its charm: a fantasy of towers and turrets, an expression of the dreams of a successful family of soldiers – the Macpherson-Grants – rather than a castle designed for defence. To the principal architect of its restoration, Thomas Mackenzie, we also owe the striking gatehouse overlooking the old bridge over the Avon.

CHAPTER 9

THE TOMINTOUL SPUR

Starting point:	**Ballindalloch Station**
Distance:	**15 miles/24.2km**
Height gained/lost:	**Gained 2200ft/674m; lost 1930ft/590m**
Time required:	**Depends on conditions, but allow 8+ hours in winter**
Car parking:	**Ballindalloch Station and Tomintoul**
Facilities:	**Shop at Brig o'An; hotels at Delnashaugh and Minmore; hotels, B&Bs, shops, toilets at Tomintoul; local museum at Tomintoul; Glenlivet Estate Outdoor Centre**
Transport:	**Enquire locally**

SUMMARY OF ROUTE

In addition to the spur to Dufftown, the Speyside Way has another to Tomintoul. From the former station at Ballindalloch the route goes to the A95 road from Grantown-on-Spey. Turning left here, you follow the A95 past the old Bridge of Avon and the imposing gates of Ballindalloch Castle, referred to above. The Way then goes past the Delnashaugh Hotel and along the B9008 road to Tomintoul for about half a mile. After passing the (former) Mill of Tormore it strikes up left past Aldich Farm on a road (soon degenerating into a track) over the west shoulder of Ben Rinnes towards Deskie Farm (OS 36-203302). Where the track divides, at a signpost, take the right-hand route in a southerly direction to its highest point to the left of

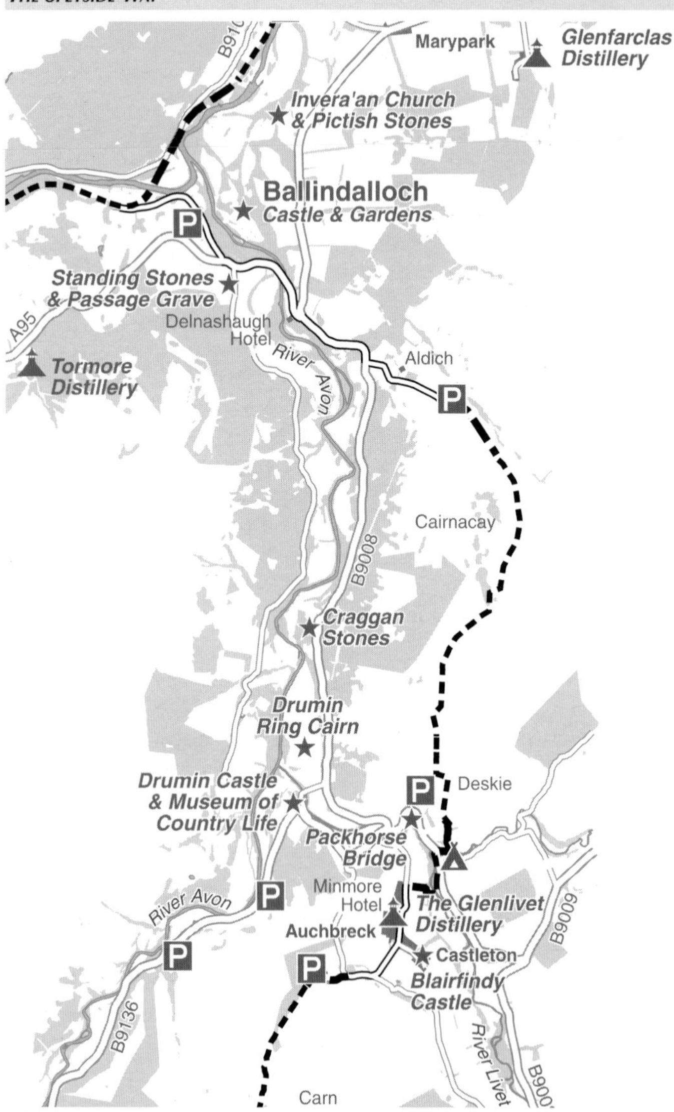

Marypark
Glenfarclas Distillery
Invera'an Church & Pictish Stones
Ballindalloch Castle & Gardens
Standing Stones & Passage Grave
A95
Delnashaugh Hotel
Tormore Distillery
River Avon
Aldich
Cairnacay
B9008
Craggan Stones
Drumin Ring Cairn
Drumin Castle & Museum of Country Life
Deskie
Packhorse Bridge
Minmore Hotel
The Glenlivet Distillery
Auchbreck
Castleton
Blairfindy Castle
B9009
River Avon
B9136
River Livet
Carn

Cairnacay Hill. All the way from Aldich the route commands views of the Scootmore Forest and Roy's Hill to the north-west of the Spey, and later of Strathavon. To the east the scene is dominated by the slopes of Ben Rinnes. As the Way descends towards Deskie, the onward route is seen, past the Glenlivet Distillery at Minmore, towards Carn Grantaich and Carn Daimh. Near the B9008 road there is a Speyside Way notice-board. The Way goes up that road for a short distance and then along a track leading to a new footbridge across the River Livet. After this a track leads to Minmore House and the legendary Glenlivet Distillery.

Leaving the distillery the Way passes Blairfindy Lodge and moves southwards over the shoulder of Carn Liath to reach its highest point in Carn Diamh (1870ft/570m). From it there is a wide panorama with attractive views north-east to Ben Rinnes, west to the Cromdale Hills, and south-west to the often snow-covered tops of Ben Avon, Ben a' Bhuird and the western Cairngorms. For many this will be the most memorable part of the Speyside Way. After this the route moves south-east to join an old right of way, the Queel or Quirn Route from Tomnavoulin to Tomintoul. Just before reaching it, a short detour might be made towards Cairn Ellick (1733ft/528m) where, if anything, the views may be even better. Returning to the 'official route' a signpost is soon met pointing left to Tomnavoulin, right to Tomintoul, and back to Ballindalloch. Taking the Tomintoul route, you soon leave the wood and follow the Speyside Way signs towards Croughly Farm. After this, the Way crosses the Conglass Burn and enters Tomintoul from the north.

GLENLIVET DISTILLERY: This distillery was born of the Illicit Distillation (Scotland) Act of 1823. This Act imposed for the umpteenth time stringent penalties for most offences connected with the unlicensed distilling of whisky, but it differed from earlier Acts both in respect of its draconian penalties and the increased powers given to the excise officers – the hated 'gaugers'. George

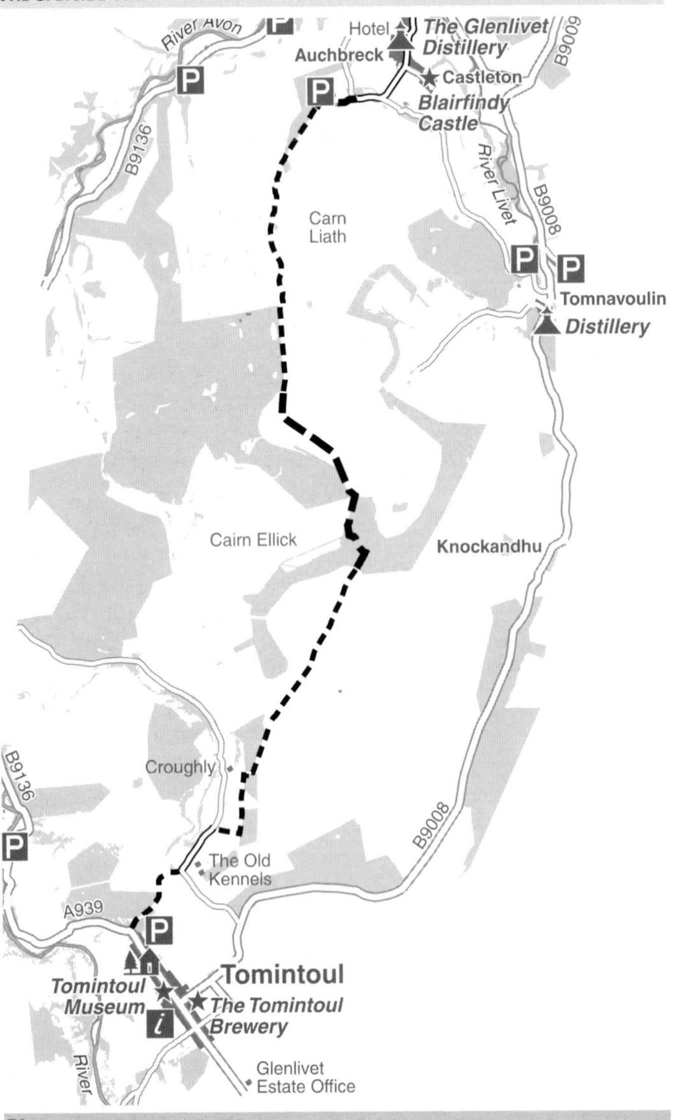
River Avon
Hotel
The Glenlivet Distillery
B9009
Auchbreck
Castleton
Blairfindy Castle
B9136
River Livet
B9008
Carn Liath
Tomnavoulin
Distillery
Cairn Ellick
Knockandhu
Croughly
B9136
B9008
The Old Kennels
A939
Tomintoul
Tomintoul Museum
The Tomintoul Brewery
River
Glenlivet Estate Office

Signpost near Cairn Ellick

Smith, a young farmer and successful unlicensed distiller at Upper Drumin, soon decided to apply for an excise. Having obtained it, he attracted the emnity of his neighbours, who threatened to burn the distillery to the ground. This had happened elsewhere. Smith responded by equipping himself with a couple of hair-trigger pistols and by employing 'two or three stout fellows' to help him keep watch, as they did for several years. Although in 1825 and 1826 three more legal distilleries were founded in the glen, they soon succumbed in the face of threats. The determined Smith eventually won through. Smith's Glenlivet – The Glenlivet – won the battle and continues today to warm the heart.

TOMINTOUL VILLAGE: Like Fochabers and Grantown-on-Spey, Tomintoul was a planned village, founded in 1776 by the fourth Duke of Gordon to create jobs in the vicinity. However, the linen and flax industries which he sought to encourage were a failure and, even with quite generous plots, the few people who settled there failed to prosper – little wonder at a height of

Drumin Castle

Below Cairn Ellick looking towards Ben Rinnes

over 1000ft/300m. The Andersons, writing in about 1850, said of Tomintoul: 'It consists of about 100 houses of, with three or four exceptions, one storey, partly slated, partly thatched with heather. They are arranged in a straight street, with a square in the centre' (G and P Anderson, *Guide to the Highlands and Islands of Scotland*, Edinburgh, 1850). Queen Victoria, despite her general enthusiasm for the Highlands, was not at all impressed when she visited the place on 5th September 1850: but her visit was on a rainy day.

In the absence of rain, Tomintoul today has much to offer those interested in outdoor pursuits. There is ski-ing at the Lecht, walking in unspoiled country, salmon fishing, and some shooting. The town lies in the Crown Estate which, with considerable success, has sought to be a model landlord, whether in the interests of farming and other tenants, or visitors. In Tomintoul Square a striking neo-classical statue was erected in 1915 by Robert Grant, M.D., as a memento of his boyhood in the village. There is a useful Tomintoul Tourist Office and museum, but a visit should also be made to the office of the Estate Ranger, near the south end of the village (tel. 0180 74283). He produces an instructive map giving a wide selection of tracks and trails in Glenlivet.

CHAPTER 10

BALLINDALLOCH TO GRANTOWN-ON-SPEY

Starting point:	**Ballindalloch Station**
Distance:	**13 miles/20.9km**
Height gained/lost:	**Gained 650ft/200m; lost 490ft/150m**
Time required:	**Ground rough at times. Allow 6+ hours**
Car parking:	**Ballindalloch, Cromdale and Grantown-on-Spey**
Facilities:	**Post office (tel. 01479 872130), Haugh Hotel (tel. 01479 872583) and shop possibly opening at Cromdale. Wide range of accommodation at Grantown-on-Spey**
Transport:	**Limited service by Highland Country Buses (tel. 01470 811211) linking Ballindalloch, Cromdale and Grantown-on-Spey**

Summary of route

There is ample parking at Ballindalloch Station and a former station building, now a private hostel, bears the name BALLINDALLOCH in bold letters. The Speyside Way now goes west along the old rail track until in 500m or so (SWS) it crosses a burn flowing from the Cragganmore Distillery, a little to the south. The route soon curves to the south-west, passing a former linesman's shelter on the way. The views here towards Craig of Callender and its grouse buts are attractive. In a short distance,

1.5 miles/2km from Ballindalloch, the rail track is blocked by fencing (SWS) and you are directed upwards to the south-east. The route is fenced on either side until it turns south-west along a squelchy route from which emissions from Tormore Distillery are seen. Tormore Distillery was built in 1959 and, though stylishly modern, fits well into the countryside. The route continues below the distillery and across the Allt an Torra Mhoir until, a short distance from the farm track from Easter Achvochkie, you meet the A95 (NJ 148355). This road is particularly busy for this area. Cross the road and follow a made path along the south side of the road until it turns up towards the west side of Garvault Plantation. Here it follows a forestry road for 600m before turning off it to the west (SWS) to cross the Garvault Burn. Ahead, an outlier of the Cromdale Hills, the Hill of Knockfrink, seems something of a barrier to further progress, but the way uses forestry tracks through the Woods of Knockfrink, emerging at a point (NJ 128324) where there are fine views over the Spey. The route then descends some 250ft/75m and turns south-west along boggy ground on which large boulders have been laid, following a route above the cultivated fields of the farm of Mains of Dalvey. The Way then descends sharply towards the Burn of Dalvey, crosses it by a bridge and meets a country road going south.

Here the planners of the Way were faced with another outlier of the Cromdale Hills, Tom an Uird and its Wood. The country road that passes Easter and Wester Rynaballoch, on its way to Cromdale, has fine views up the Spey Valley, and offers frequent sightings of pheasants and grouse and occasional views of roe deer. This route is used as a temporary deviation at present since access has not as yet been obtained to a small section of the 'official' route which follows old forestry tracks to the north and west of Tom an Uird Wood. The 'official' route eventually emerges at the south-west corner of this wood near the A95, crosses it and regains the railway trackbed a little south of Pollowick. The trackbed is then followed to a point on the

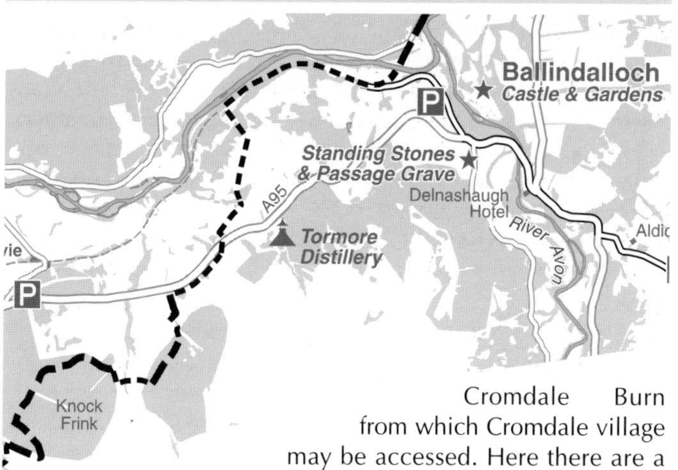

Cromdale Burn from which Cromdale village may be accessed. Here there are a hotel and a post office. If you do not wish to visit the village the trackbed may be followed to the site of the former Cromdale Station.

The Speyside Way then moves north-west along the minor road from Cromdale to its parish church. This has a poignant notice relating to the Battle of Cromdale in 1690. Between the church and the road stands a venerable beech tree, the ancestor of which was said by the writer of the New Statistical Account to be capable of sheltering a thousand men. There used to be a ferry across the Spey beside the church, which is reflected in such names as Boat of Cromdale. Later there was a light foot suspension bridge. Nowadays, the Speyside Way crosses the river by an old metal bridge from which there are attractive views both up and down the river.

On the west side of the bridge, a good track along the west side of the river appears on the left. Joining it through a metal gate, a path appears (SWS) running along the north-west side of a small burn. This is followed for about 500m until it meets a good track to the right. The route, however, goes to the left over a cattle grid. Very soon a path to the right appears with a fence and stile (SWS). The Way then follows a meandering track through superb pine woods with accompanying birch trees and the ground cover common to this part of the country. On a sunny day the views of changing light and shade are attractive. The wood used to be home to the capercailzie (highland wood cock). They are less often seen today, but smaller birds and butterflies lend interest to the walk. After some 500m from the stile, the path bifurcates and you take the route to the left. When a choice of route seems to be offered later, take the track to the right. (It is possible that near this point you will meet a group of young people engaged in an orienteering competition – the place is used by a local RAF School of Physical Training. It seems that not all their training consists of 20 mile expeditions to the Cairngorm summits and other commando-like trials of endurance.) Eventually, the path leads to Grantown-on-Spey golf course where a small wicket gate gives access to a tarmaced road

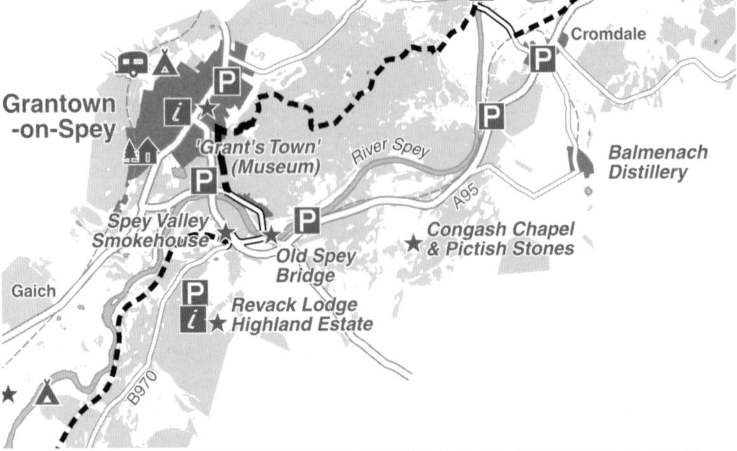

through the golf course, which leads to the town. Grantown-on-Spey has many attractions and should certainly be visited. At the gate, however, an SWS indicates that the Speyside Way turns left in a southerly and westerly direction until it meets Forest Road (SWS). Follow this road south until it meets a road bearing left (SWS), initially along the banks of the Spey, towards Old Speybridge. An SWS at the south side of the bridge directs you to the next section of the Way, leading to Nethy Bridge.

When leaving the town to continue the Way towards Nethy Bridge, aim for the south-west corner of the Square and turn left along Forest Road, which soon moves south through pleasant woodland running parallel to and east of the A95. Where Forest Road meets the road along the banks of the Spey it is equally possible to turn right to join the A95 and cross over the (New) Speybridge. Continue past the Spey Valley Smokehouse to the B970 where in a matter of yards Speyside Way signs direct you to the route to Nethy Bridge.

CROMDALE: The Haughs of Cromdale is an area once famed for long forgotten battles now celebrated in locally popular songs. Overlooking the haughs are the somewhat bleak Cromdale Hills. They are of no great height – 2330ft/710m at the highest point – but impose an effective barrier between Speyside and Glen Avon. Cromdale was once quite a centre of illicit distilling and long ago there were frequent skirmishes between desperate smugglers and the gaugers. The former led their ponies at dead of night, burdened with ankers of precious liquid, over the Cromdale Hills into Strath Avon and on to markets in the south. In the early 19th century two Macgregor brothers settled in Cromdale and another, James Macgregor, above Cromdale. No doubt, like his neighbours, he supplemented his income by making a smidgeon of unlicensed whisky. Being a realist, however, he eventually succumbed to the law and in 1824 the chimneys of the Balmenach Distillery began to reek. Rapidly, its quality became appreciated, particularly in the

Cromdale Station

north-east of Scotland. Once the Speyside line reached Cromdale, Balmenach Distillery was visited by Alfred Barnard, who describes the occasion with pleasure. He particularly enjoyed being shown round the remains of illicit stills nearby and hearing the account of at least one battle with discomfited gaugers. The distillery itself appealed more to his interest in the antiquarian and picturesque than the practical: 'Like all other parts of this establishment the building [the still house] and its contents are of the most antiquated type. Never did we see such picturesque pot stills and vessels as are to be seen in this ancient Distillery' (Barnard, p223). Antiquated though the distillery may have been, its product was much appreciated by Queen Victoria, and in 1897 it was one of the first to build its own railway siding, now dismantled. After a recent period of closure, the distillery has resumed working, retaining traditional methods but exuding an air of business-like efficiency.

GRANTOWN-ON-SPEY: Grantown-on-Spey is a fine example of a planned village. The local laird, Sir James Grant of Grant, advertised for settlers in the Aberdeen Journal of 15th April 1765, explaining that the proposed location was near to the Spey Bridge and had roads branching off from it to Inverness, Elgin, Keith, Perth and elsewhere. He vaunted the 'good, pleasant country', the sources of fuel, the place's suitability for wool or linen manufacture, and the availability of wood which for a very moderate price could be floated down the Spey to Garmouth. The town was planned on the grid system. The old market place became the Square, through which the main road ran, with lesser roads parallel to it. The Square is spacious – 700 by 108ft/213 by 33m – with swards of green grass and set off by pleasant trees. Largish feus were given off and some care was taken to ensure that the feuars were artisans or merchants likely to succeed. The estate itself provided a 'neat and commodious schoolhouse' towards the north side of the town. By the 1780s the venture had succeeded and the town was rapidly becoming the commercial centre of upper Speyside. In around 1830 several banks had branches there, and there were handsome churches of various denominations. Though the woollen trade prospered, the linen trade did not survive the coming of cotton after the Napoleonic wars.

But a new 'industry' was soon to benefit Grantown-on-Spey. In 1860 Queen Victoria stayed incognito for one night at the Grant Arms Hotel on the south side of the Square and maintained the deception till morning. As she says, 'When they heard who it was, they were ready to drop with astonishment and fright'. Despite several vicissitudes the Grant Arms Hotel still entertains visitors. Following the arrival of the Highland line and the Speyside Railway in 1863, Grantown-on-Spey could take a share of the growing tourist traffic. The tourists required accommodation, which the citizens of the town were none too proud to offer. The train journey from the south was long, and possibly tiring, but in early summer the middle-class burghers of Edinburgh, Glasgow and Dundee were prepared to leave their offices and counting houses for the invigorating air and country walks in the pine woods near Grantown-on-Spey, and for the fishing on the Spey. A different class of tourist came for the grouse shooting in August and, later in the autumn, others for the stalking and a late run of salmon.

This pattern continued until cheap flights in the 1950s to far-flung places gave British tourists a taste for holidays abroad. Grantown-on-Spey became impoverished until ski-ing started in Speyside in the 1960s. Apart from facilities for ski-ing on the slopes of Cairngorm in the spring, Grantown-on-Spey now has many attractions. Still at its heart is the spacious Square with several buildings which catch the eye. It has a pleasant golf course, arguably the best on Speyside, and a museum. It is also the planned terminus of the new Speyside Railway, which will give to the young and not so young the chance of a journey by lovingly restored steam trains to and from Aviemore and Boat of Garten.

While at Grantown-on-Spey, or when leaving it, a pleasant visit may be made to the Old Spey Bridge. This was built in 1754, by the orders of Major Caulfield, as part of the military road from Braemar, via the Lecht and Tomintoul, to Fort George. The deck is on a slope because the south or right bank is rather higher. The bridge is well finished and substantial and is quite a testimony to the E Companies of the 33 RD Regiment who built it and left a simple but proud memorial to their achievement.

Chapter 11

GRANTOWN-ON-SPEY TO AVIEMORE

Starting point:	**South-west corner of Grantown Square**
Distance:	**17 miles/27km**
Height gained/lost:	**Insignificant**
Time required:	**Allowing for diversions, 8 hours**
Car parking:	**Grantown-on-Spey, Nethy Bridge, Boat of Garten, Loch Garten and Aviemore**
Facilities:	**Hotels, B&Bs, shop, post office, toilets in Nethy Bridge, Boat of Garten and Aviemore**
Transport:	**Highland Country Buses – Aviemore, Boat of Garten, Nethy Bridge, Grantown-on-Spey and Tormore. Speyside Steam Railway from Boat of Garten to Aviemore**

Summary of Route

The next section of the Speyside Way commences on the B970 road shortly after that road leaves the A95, not far from the Spey Valley Smokehouse. The Way follows the track of the old railway, heading directly for Nethy Bridge, less than 3.5 miles/6km away. For the first 2 miles/3km it follows the course of the Spey, with pleasant views of the river and of the hills north of Dulnain Bridge and Carr Bridge. The earlier part of the route goes in and out of small pine woods, with knolls and hillocks suggesting that it may have formed part of the terminal moraine of a large glacier. At two or three places bridges over the old railway survive, notably near Boat of Balliefurth and at Balliefurth Farm. Near the former an attractive modern house has been built, with fine views over the river. Approaching Nethy Bridge the track goes under electricity transmission lines. Nearby are the ruins of Castle Roy, held by the Comyns, when Lords of Badenoch. Sadly, little of its history survives.

The Speyside Way reaches Nethy Bridge at the site of its former station. Here the Way leaves the track of the former Speyside line. The route moves south-west across the old bridge (see below), and a new track alongside the B970 public road is followed to reach (SWS) an unclassified road to Tulloch and Loch Garten. A short distance along this road the Way takes a track on the right (SWS), first going north-west and then south-west. The route soon reaches a line of electricity pylons which is followed by a newly made track for about half a mile, and later (SWS) this new track turns south-west to meet a forest road coming from Loch Garten. Here the Way, turning right, continues on a made path to the left of this road in the direction of East Croftamore, where the path now moves beside the B970 until a link road turns directly west towards the bridge over the Spey at Boat of Garten.

This village is now reasonably provided with hotel and other accommodation, shops and even a small golf course with attractive views of the Spey and of the distant Cairngorms. The growth of the 'the Boat' as an Edwardian holiday resort was

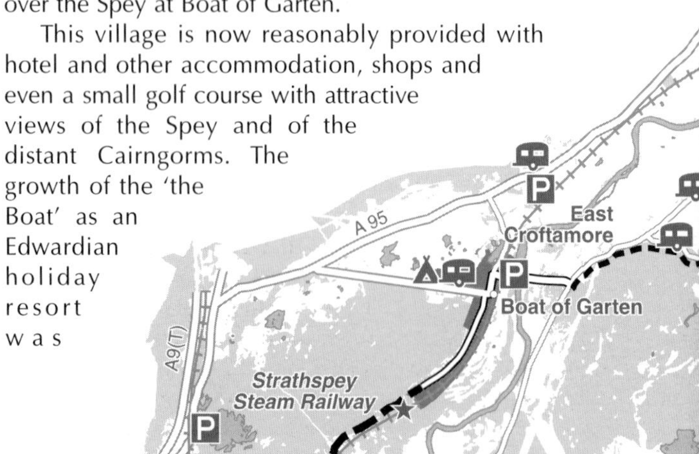

entirely due to the presence of the railway. The old Speyside Railway went no further than 'the Boat', and the railway onwards was run by the Highland line.

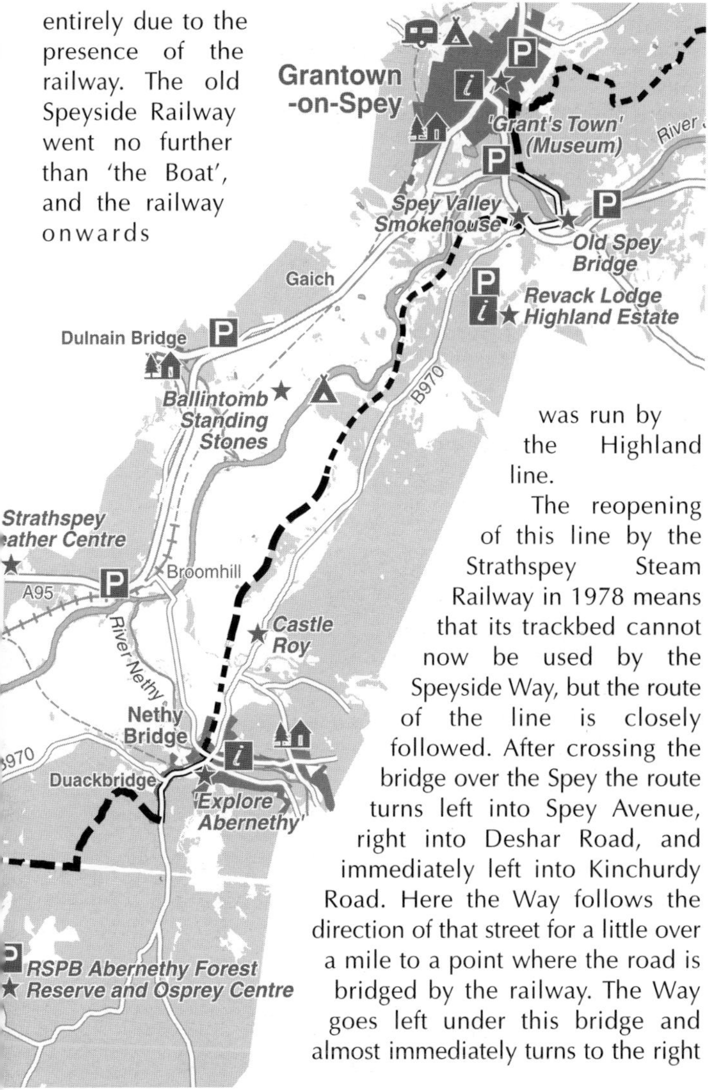

The reopening of this line by the Strathspey Steam Railway in 1978 means that its trackbed cannot now be used by the Speyside Way, but the route of the line is closely followed. After crossing the bridge over the Spey the route turns left into Spey Avenue, right into Deshar Road, and immediately left into Kinchurdy Road. Here the Way follows the direction of that street for a little over a mile to a point where the road is bridged by the railway. The Way goes left under this bridge and almost immediately turns to the right

(SWS) along an improved track on the east side of, and close to, the line. As the track approaches the Dalfaber development north of Aviemore signs direct you west towards the B91652 and then south to Aviemore Railway Station where the Speyside Way ends or, as the case may be, begins.

NETHY BRIDGE: There is a variety of accommodation in or near Nethy Bridge, and you may wish to visit the Explore Abernethy Centre to learn about the district and the network of paths which is being developed in the vicinity. The centre is in Dell Road, turning left immediately after the bridge.

This bridge across the River Nethy gives its name to the village. It is a listed building and has clearly been extensively repaired. Dick Lauder describes the scene on 4/5th August 1829:

> *'Terror and confusion spread fast among the inhabitants at Bridge of Nethy... At about eight o'clock [in the morning] a number of people were standing in the middle of it, wondering at the immensity and the roaring of the river that was carrying down large trees, and tossing them up perpendicularly, when all at once the enormous mass of timber building composing the saw-mill of Straanbeg, about 500 yards above, moved bodily off, steadily and magnificently, like some three-decker leaving dock. On it came grandly, without a plank being dislodged. It was tremendous – it was awful to see it advancing on the bridge. Some moved quickly away... destruction seemed inevitable, when all at once it struck a bulwark, went to pieces with a fearful crash... But the river, having once breached through beyond its western land-breast, undermined it on the flank, [and] swept away the western arch'* (T D Lauder, *The Great Floods of 1829 in the Province of Moray*, 3rd edn, 1873, p106).

The Nethy, even today, can become a forceful river. It has its source at 2650ft/807m just east of Cairngorm on the saddle between it and Ben Bynack, a place in the heart of the Cairngorms with dramatic views up Loch Avon and towards Ben Mheadhoin. The Nethy starts as the small

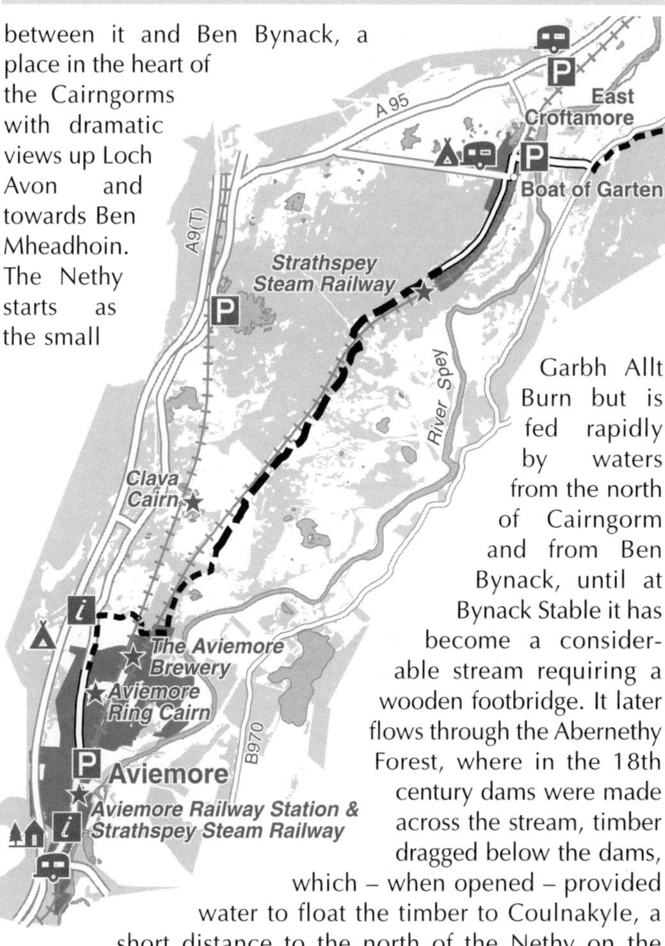

Garbh Allt Burn but is fed rapidly by waters from the north of Cairngorm and from Ben Bynack, until at Bynack Stable it has become a considerable stream requiring a wooden footbridge. It later flows through the Abernethy Forest, where in the 18th century dams were made across the stream, timber dragged below the dams, which – when opened – provided water to float the timber to Coulnakyle, a short distance to the north of the Nethy on the Broomhill road. Coulnakyle is now a farmstead, apparently designed in 1765 by John Adam, and is a listed building. Coulnakyle in the early 18th century was the main focus of the operations of the York Buildings Company, and housed its busy

Castle Roy on the way to Nethy Bridge

saw mills and iron ore smelters. Shortly after Coulnakyle the road leads to a bridge across the Spey at Broomhill (NH 997223). This must be one of the last wooden road bridges to span such a wide river. It makes a fine sight with its 15 spans and may be viewed from a riverside path.

LOCH GARTEN: It is possible to divert from the Way and visit Loch Garten by turning left when you meet the forest road to the loch. Loch Garten is a secluded and delightful spot in the depths of the Abernethy Forest. Here the Royal Society for the Protection of Birds (RSPB), consolidating the success of a few dedicated enthusiasts, has a visitor centre. This permits members of the public to view in its nesting season that remarkable fish-eating hawk, the osprey, as well as other attractive species such as crested tits, crossbills, golden plovers and, possibly, caper-cailzies. The osprey was originally not uncommon in Scotland, but its beauty and relative rarity brought it to the attention of persons who wanted a stuffed bird as a trophy or who collected birds' eggs. Ospreys were not known to have bred in Scotland after 1916. The story is vividly recounted by George Waterston in *The Return of the Osprey* (Philip Brown and G Waterston, London, 1962). Ospreys resumed nesting in Scotland in 1954 at Loch Garten, but nest robberies continued until, after careful protective measures by the RSPB, a pair successfully raised three young in 1959. The RSPB created a visitor centre and installed a hide from which, during the nesting period, the birds might be viewed. It is thought that as many as 2 million people have visited the centre in the last 40 years. In 1999, at a cost of £250,000, the RSPB opened a new Osprey Centre with facilities for viewing the nesting ospreys and local pine-forest birds by closed-circuit television. These facilities should enhance the experience of visitors and, possibly, attract more than the 50,000 to 60,000 visitors now coming annually to the site. Loch Garten is no longer a haven of peace and tranquillity, but it may be that the visible presence of ospreys here serves to protect them in other localities.

BOAT OF GARTEN: The name Boat of Garten derives from the former ferry at this place, latterly a chain-operated one, replaced by a bridge in 1899. The loss of the ferry was regretted by the romantically inclined who were prepared to watch the leisurely loading of a few vehicles on one side of the river and their equally leisurely unloading on the other. Shortly after the bridge, there appears on the left the home of the Strathspey Railway Association. Its members, starting in the mid seventies, took over engines and rolling stock with a view to restoring railway services to Aviemore. Thanks to lots of enthusiasm and hard work their initial aim has been fulfilled and, in the summer months, the Association has an imaginative programme of events, including an excursion by train (with dining car) hauled by a steam engine to Aviemore. The train journey is a delight to children of all ages and affords spectacular views successively of Cairngorm and its corries, the Lairig Ghru, and of Braeriach and its corries. Boat of Garten is now reasonably provided with hotel and other accommodation, shops and a small golf course with attractive views of the Spey and the distant Cairngorms.

AVIEMORE: Aviemore, consisting (as the village once did) of little more than the railway station and an adjacent hotel, received the barest of mentions in George and Peter Anderson's *Guide to the Inverness and Nairn Railway* (Inverness, 1856), but the writers did speak of Loch Balladron – now named Balladern – then the habitat of the smallest and rarest of British water-lilies *(Nuphar minima),* and referred to the hill Craigellachie above and to the west of Aviemore as being literally covered with cranberry and many interesting woodland and alpine plants.

Aviemore is very different today, being one of the busier and more successful holiday resorts in Scotland. It now possesses every category of hotel, B&B, hostel, self-catering accommodation, time-share, and caravan parks. It has bars, cafes and bistros and, in the view of some, offers the most vivid après-ski in Europe. The hotels and tourist association do their best to attract visitors throughout the year and to that end arrange conferences and events of every kind. Inevitably, an artificial ski slope is joined by an ice-rink, squash courts, a go-kart track and shopping facilities. But the raison d'être of Aviemore now is the winter and spring ski-ing on the slopes of Cairngorm. Those used to the effete comforts and sunshine of the alpine resorts of Europe will find it tough and demanding, very tough when the winter winds are blowing fiercely across the slopes, but glorious when in late May, or even in June, spring snow permits long runs from the summit of Cairngorm nearly to the forests below. In other seasons the town of Aviemore is easily left for the dramatic views at Loch Morlich or Loch Inch, or for the charms of Loch an Eilein or of Loch Pityoulish. Do not forget, however, that little gem of a hill, Craigellachie. A useful leaflet about it is available at the tourist information centre.

Towards Coire an Lochain (Chapter 11)

From Loch an Eilein: G.F. Robson's soft etching of 1819 (Chapter 11)

Malt stills at Cnoc Distillery (Appendix)

Auchroisk: a modern distillery near Boat O'Brig (Appendix and Chapter 5)

CRAIGELLACHIE: The hill lies to the west of the A9 and is approached via a tunnel under this road. Take the road from the main street to the Aviemore Centre and head for the car park beyond the Badenoch Hotel near the dry ski slope. A path leaves the road and heads for the west side of the lochan below the A9. This path is followed to, and through, the tunnel. After this the path continues in a westerly direction until it divides. Either route may be followed, but that to the left takes you on a pleasant clockwise track round the nature trail. Although provided in various places with stone steps it gives little impression of artificiality. There are no obtrusive numbered posts. Where the track begins to turn downhill, a subsidiary path may be taken upwards to a higher viewpoint. From here, when the weather is favourable, there are excellent views of Loch Morlich and Cairngorm, with its ski-slopes and corries. Coire an' Sneachda and Coire Lochan come into view and there are glimpses towards the Lairig Ghru and Braeriach. Returning to the main path, the route descends through heather, blaeberries and cranberries, with a few rowans and mixed trees until it enters a charming area of natural birch trees. The distinctive wildlife on Craigellachie led to part of it being declared a National Nature Reserve. The presence of peregrine falcons means that visitors are asked not to stray from the paths during their nesting season, particularly between April and July. But many smaller species of bird are to be seen, including finches, wagtails, wrens and siskins.

ROTHIEMURCHUS ESTATE AND LOCH AN EILEIN: The Rothiemurchus Highland Estate is central to outdoor activities near Aviemore. Its Visitor Centre (tel. 01479 812345) on the Cairngorm Ski Road near to the B970 gives advice on the walking, cycling and mountain biking routes in the estate, on guided walks, on safari and 4*4 tours, trout fishing and other activities. One of the more popular excursions is to Loch an Eilein (the Loch of the Island), less than three miles from

Aviemore. The road to Cairngorm is followed to Inverdruie, where a right turn is taken to join the B970 road. The first branch road to the left is then taken to a visitors' car park, and from here it is a short walk to the Visitor Centre.

Do not write off Loch an Eilein as another tourist trap. Of course it is a victim of its own charms, but these are considerable, and the loch continues to delight visitors, young and old, and to cause many to return there year after year. It has every element of the romantic Scottish scene: a ruined castle on an island, in former times the stronghold of a robber baron, the Wolf of Badenoch, who destroyed Elgin Cathedral. In more recent times the castle was one of the last nesting places of the persecuted osprey. The loch is surrounded by massive Scots pines, overlooked by hills to the west and south-west, themselves dwarfed by the outliers of Sgoran Dubh, in turn overlooked by the massifs of Braeriach and Cairngorm, so often covered in snow. But the loch is not merely the haunt of artists and photographers. There is an interesting nature trail which circles the loch and the adjacent Loch Gamhna (The Loch of the Stirks, apparently pronounced Loch Gowan). While walking along the sides of the lochs the cries of black-headed gulls can usually be heard, but there is a chance also of seeing mallards, wigeons, mergansers and other ducks. You may also see, particularly if you leave the lochside, such birds as crossbills, crested tits, woodcock and buzzards. You may even see, before they leave for sunnier climes, osprey fishing on the lochs. There are, of course, rabbits, brown hares and mountain hares and, if you are lucky, red squirrels and badgers.

Ord Ban (428m) is a conical hill immediately west of the Visitor Centre. There the nearby track to Ord Ban can be pointed out. Its rocks being basic in character, the hill supports, as well as Scots pine, silver birches, juniper, broom, bilberry, cranberry and many smaller plants.The upper part of the hill is mainly of heather, and from its simple cairn there is an excellent view of Carn Eilrig, Braeriach, the Lairig Ghru, Loch Morlich and the corries of Cairngorm. In earlier days, at least, a group of red deer hinds frequented Ord Ban. You are unlikely to see night-hunting species such as the fox or the wild-cat, though apparently the latter had a lair in byegone days on Kennepole Hill, which lies west of Loch Gamhna. This hill may be approached by walking along the lochside until a farm is reached and from there aiming to tackle the hill from its south-west flank. Kennepole Hill is itself an excellent viewpoint and was frequented by the Duchess of Bedford, herself daughter of the famed Lady Jane Maxwell, Duchess of Gordon. There is a moving tribute to the former on the top of Kennepole:

To her whose eye explored
And whose step marked
With discriminating taste
This little path
From Loch Gamhna to the
Cat's den and round
The Craig of Kinnepole
To its Summit
This simple tablet is inscribed
By a sincere and affectionate friend.

AVIEMORE – THE FUTURE: At the time of writing, extensive plans are under consideration for touristic developments in or around Aviemore. The planned creation of a funicular railway on the slopes of Cairngorm attracted criticism from various environmental bodies, but this development has now won the snakes-and-ladders game of planning permissions. Tourist interests regard it as crucial to the future of Aviemore. Barratt International Resorts have submitted an application to create an 18-hole golf course and clubhouse near their existing complex at Dalfaber village. The Aviemore Partnership, which brings together a variety of local interests, has welcomed an application by Aviemore Mountain Resort for their creation of 120 new holiday homes and chalets there. Though many will regret these proposals, the atmosphere of the old village of Aviemore was lost, and lost forever, long, long ago.

NATIONAL PARK PROPOSALS

Finally, the current proposals for the Cairngorms National Park may be mentioned. Similar proposals have often been made in the past, but it was not until the National Parks (Scotland) Act was enacted in 2000 that a legislative vehicle was provided for the designation of national parks in Scotland. In September 2000 Scottish Ministers decided to consider, in addition to proposals for national parks in the Trossachs and Loch Lomond area, the case for a national park in the Cairngorms and to appoint Scottish Natural Heritage (SNH) as Reporter. SNH were required as Reporter to make a written proposal and to undertake consultation process upon it. Their main constraint was the Scottish Ministers' preference for the planning function to rest with the local authorities. The SNH proposal was published in December 2000 and the public was invited to comment on the proposal by 13th April 2001. It seems inappropriate in a guide to walkers to comment on such key questions as the boundaries of the park and the division of planning powers. It may be said, however, that the merits of the SNH proposal as to substance, and its skilful presentation of complex issues, augur well for the future of the Cairngorms National Park.

APPENDIX

SPEY WHISKY

Many books have been written about the romance of scotch whisky, and it is not intended here to add to this remarkable collection. One is reminded of J Fennimore Cooper's Last of the Mohicans where the sympathies of readers tend to move from the Palefaces to the Redskins – we know that the Redskins could be savagely cruel, but feel perhaps that they had no alternative faced by the threat of the Palefaces to their whole way of life. The small farmers and crofters in the upland districts of Scotland in the 17th and early 18th centuries faced lives of considerable hardship. Famines were not unknown and, in times without famine, they could pay their rent only with cash from the sale of barley to local distillers or themselves making and selling whisky. The flouting of the savage excise laws of the time had become a moral imperative for the farmer who wished to retain his croft and feed his family. But his whisky had to be sold in the south and the whisky smugglers, faced by the excise men, or 'gaugers' as they were called, became wild and desperate men who risked their own and the gaugers' lives to carry their precious ankers of whisky to the south and who, in doing so, became local heroes. After the Excise Act of 1823 illicit distilling gradually disappeared and, with it, the pitched battles with gaugers. The romance of scotch whisky came to be found rather in the skills of the men who made it. Though the external appearance of some of the older distilleries may be preserved, most of the whisky is now produced in bulk in factories owned by large concerns using the best in modern science and the latest in modern technology. Since Speyside is par excellence the home of the Scottish malt whisky industry, visits to such of the distilleries as are on or adjacent to the Speyside Way may add to the interest of the route.

One of the first, and today probably the most famous of the lawful distilleries set up after the Act of 1823, was that established by George Smith, tenant of Upper Drumin Farm. In his speech in the House of Lords advocating the passing of the Act, the Duke of Gordon had stressed that highland tenants could not easily pay their rents without being able to sell their barley to the distillers. So when the Act was passed the Duke's factor at Drumin, James Skinner, recommended to all his tenants with the means of doing so to set up stills. But few had suitable buildings and in the district two who had begun distilling found it impossible to continue. George Smith, too, was in a rather parlous financial state, but Skinner persuaded Smith to sell his cattle and farm plenishings so that he might concentrate on distilling. He assisted Smith in securing a settlement with his creditors and sufficient finance. Skinner then made strenuous efforts to build up a market for the whisky among the nobility and among his discerning professional acquaintance in the south.

Speyside remains even today the home of the best regarded Scottish malt distilleries. For practical reasons only those not too far from the Speyside Way will be mentioned and especially those which admit visitors. The Way runs briefly through the Minmore Distillery which now produces The Glenlivet. It continues to maintain its excellent reputation though it has several rivals. Among them is its sister distillery at Rothes, which produces Glen Grant. Both are popular world-wide and equally so is Glenfiddich, produced in Dufftown. These are de luxe whiskies, and with them must be mentioned Glenfarclas, produced at a distillery not far from Ballindalloch Castle, and The Macallan, produced at Easter Elchies, just across the Spey from Craigellachie. In recent years The Macallan has become a whisky of exceptional repute. It is still matured in sherry casks, and it continues to use small stills modelled on those of long ago.

MAKING MALT WHISKY

There are five main stages in the process of making malt whisky, namely: malting the barley, mashing or extracting the maltose from the malted barley, fermenting the product, distilling it, and maturing the whisky.

MALTING THE BARLEY

The malting stage has changed the most in recent times. In former days barley, often from farms in the vicinity, was delivered to a local distillery where it was checked for quality and humidity, cleaned and graded. After this it was soaked and softened in water for two or three days in big tanks called 'steeps'. The surplus water was then run off and the moist barley spread on level floors for seven days, more or less, to germinate. It was usually spread quite thickly at first and the barley soon began to sprout or develop tiny roots. This caused the barley to heat. To even out its temperature to around 16°C and to prevent the roots matting, the barley was turned over by the maltmen and spread more thinly on the floor. During germination the enzymes in the barley break down the starches in the grain into maltose, a soluble sugar. The germination process was then stopped by further heating the germinated barley in a controlled way up to some 70°C. After this, traditionally, the damp malted barley was laid quite deeply on a heated floor to dry and exposed to peat smoke sufficient to give the whisky the slightly peaty flavour characteristic of the particular distillery. Until fully dried the malted barley was occasionally turned to ensure an even exposure to the peat smoke. The sprouts fell off during the drying process and were then removed. The dried barley, now 'malted barley', was now almost ready for the next stage. The malting process described above is called the 'former process' because most – but not all – malt distilleries now purchase the malted barley from specialised 'maltings', which are located at Buckie, Burghead and elsewhere.

MASHING

When the malted barley is delivered from the maltings it receives certain quality checks and then is passed to a grist mill to be ground, not too finely, before it is soaked in a huge vessel called a 'mash tun'. This is fitted with revolving rakes (or stirrers) and hot water is introduced, possibly first at 65°C, later at one or two successively higher temperatures, and finally it is soaked at about 90°C. This process extracts the sugars (maltose) from the grists. The products of this process are a sweet liquid – the wort – and solid residues or draff, the latter of which is removed from the mash tun and sold for cattle feed. The draff has quite a strong smell, which is a clue to the existence of a distillery nearby. The wort from the first two soakings is cooled to around 21–26°C and poured into the fermenting tuns. The weaker wort from later soakings goes back again into a mash tun for a later soaking with grist, called 'mashing in'.

FERMENTING

The sweet liquor (or wort) from the first two soakings of grist is transferred to huge fermenting tuns called 'wash-backs', a measured amount of yeast is added and the fermentation process begins. It is quite vigorous and to prevent the froth spilling over, revolving blades are used to deactivate it. The products of the fermenting process are alcohol at seven to eight per cent, and carbon dioxide. When, after 46 hours or so, the distiller concludes that the process has gone on long enough, the fermented liquor or wash goes to a pot still to be distilled.

DISTILLING

In the making of malt whisky the shape of the stills is all important. There are two kinds of still but both depend on the fact that alcohol evaporates at a lower temperature than water. The larger is the wash still where the liquor is heated to cause the alcohol in the fermented liquor to evaporate. Older illustrations show the stills being heated by a blazing peat or coal fire. This could scorch elements in the liquor and possibly alter the taste of the final product. Many stills, therefore, are now heated by internal steam coils. The vapour is then condensed through coils cooled by cold water. The liquor, now called 'low wines' (at about 17 per cent alcohol), is transferred to what is called a 'low wines charger' for temporary storage. It later goes to a second and smaller pot still for what is in principle its final distillation.

Not all of the distillate is used. The first part of the distillate is called 'foreshots', which contain lighter alcohols rather than the ethyl alcohol required for whisky. The foreshots, therefore, or 'head', is redirected to the low wines charger for reuse. The last part of the distillate, or 'tail', may contain heavier elements, such as fusel oil, found to be undesirable in a quality product. This part, again, is redirected to the low wines charger. The central part, or 'heart', comes out of the still at some 66 per cent alcohol. In distinguishing between the foreshots, the heart and the tail lies the art of the stillman. He is assisted in this by tests, such as for specific gravity and impurities, which he can carry out in what is called the 'spirit safe'. This was formerly padlocked and under the charge of the excise man. Now, however, the spirit duty is not assessed by the theoretical throughput of the stills but at the time of bottling. Today, therefore, the padlocking becomes part of a management control system to satisfy excise requirements.

MATURING

The final stage in the manufacture of malt whisky is its maturation. By law it is required to be kept for at least three years in oak casks. In the past, and still today by The Macallan, old sherry casks were used. More commonly the casks are imported from the United States where they have been used in the maturation of Kentucky Bourbon. The new spirit is not poured directly into the casks: it is first diluted to 111 degrees proof or 63.5 per cent volume using water from the source used earlier

The still room at Glenfarcas Distillery

in the distilling process. This is reckoned to be the best strength to begin the process of maturation. Whisky, unlike wine, does not mature once bottled: it matures only in the cask, so that the date of bottling the whisky should not be a selling point. It would be different if the bottle bore, as some do, both the date of distillation and the date of bottling. Though chemists could no doubt explain how it is that whisky matures in the cask, it is customary – and much safer – to refer to a number of factors: chemical, climatic and the nature of the casks themselves. If they are old sherry casks they will add colour to the hitherto colourless spirit and in some small degree affect its flavour. The casks, too, are slightly porous and allow the spirit to be affected by the local air and climate and allow outwards evaporation. The loss by evaporation is quite significant, say two per cent a year. At any rate, with aging in the cask, malt whisky is transformed from a rather fiery liquid to one that is mellow, smooth and rich.

It seems unnecessary to make suggestions as to how to drink malt whisky. Its magical properties are there for each to discover. The anxiety of distillers to preserve the unique aromas and flavours of their products was explained originally by their anxiety to appeal to a variety of tastes. It may now be justified also by the need for the product to remain true to its original style for blending purposes. So, after tasting one or two whiskies, do not give up too easily: the palate may require to be educated. Do not start with a strongly peated malt whisky; start rather with a lighter malt such as The Singleton (of Achroisk). From that, venture further into malts with a gradually increasing 'bite', such as Cardhu, An Cnoc, Aultmore, Glenfarclas, The Macallan, Speyburn and The Glenlivet. The list could be lengthened and many others deserve to be included. Take only a small sip of each whisky with a little spring water and, between each whisky, clear the palate with a small chunk of a hard cheese of your choice. Your palate will have started its Early Learning course... And finally, the Gaelic toast to your good health: Slainte' Mhath.

FURTHER READING

A detailed book list would be out of place. Extensive use was made of the Old Statistical Account (1794) and the New Statistical Account (c.1845), but these are readily obtainable only in University and Public Libraries. The more recent *The Moray Book* (Edinburgh, 1976) and *The Grampian Book* (Edinburgh, 1981) are also valuable, but lack the personal immediacy of the Statistical Accounts.

Thomas Dick Lauder's *The Great Floods of August 1829* (3rd edn. 1873) is much more than a description of the floods: it is also a window into a way of life long since vanished. The same may be said of Mrs. Elizabeth Grant's *Memoirs of a Highland Lady* (1827, but reprinted). Francis Thompson's *Portrait of the Spey* (Edinburgh, 1979) is readable and well-informed. Peter F. Anson's *Fishing Boats and Fishing Folk on the East Coast of Scotland* (Dent, 1971) is knowledgeable and has charming illustrations.

Many local books make interesting reading, including Geo. Hutcheson's *Days of Yore* (Buckie, 1887), G. Anderson's *Kingston-on-Spey* (Edinburgh, 1957), Jim Skelton's *Speybuilt...a Forgotten Industry* (Elgin, 1994 and 1995), Ian Hustwick's *Moray Firth Ships and Trade* (Aberdeen, 1994), G. Dunnett's *Invera'an: A Speyside Parish* (Paisley, I919), Sir Edward H. Peck's, *Avonside Explored* (Tomintoul, 1983), Victor Gaffney's *Tomintoul, its Glens and its People* (Sutherland Press, 1976*),* and H. MacMillan's *Rothiemurchus* (London, 1907). There are several books about Speyside railways and, if one must be chosen, Dick Jackson's *The Speyside Line* (Aberdeen, 1996) calls for a mention. There are innumerable books about the romance of Scotch malt whisky, but Alfred Barnard's *The Whisky Distilleries of the United Kingdom* (1887, reprinted 1969) remains unequalled.

The Speyside Way (2000) by Jacquetta Megarry and Jim Strachan, published in the Rucksack Readers series, is admirably presented and the illustrations are superb.

FOR YOUR NOTES

LISTING OF CICERONE GUIDES

NORTHERN ENGLAND LONG DISTANCE TRAILS

THE DALES WAY
THE ISLE OF MAN COASTAL PATH
THE PENNINE WAY
THE ALTERNATIVE COAST TO COAST
NORTHERN COAST-TO-COAST WALK
THE RELATIVE HILLS OF BRITAIN
MOUNTAINS ENGLAND & WALES VOL 1 WALES. VOL 2 ENGLAND.

CYCLING

BORDER COUNTRY BIKE ROUTES
THE CHESHIRE CYCLE WAY
THE CUMBRIA CYCLE WAY
THE DANUBE CYCLE WAY
LANDS END TO JOHN O'GROATS CYCLE GUIDE
ON THE RUFFSTUFF - 84 Bike Rides in Nth Engl'd
RURAL RIDES No.1 WEST SURREY
RURAL RIDES No.1 EAST SURREY
SOUTH LAKELAND CYCLE RIDES
THE WAY OF ST JAMES Le Puy to Santiago - Cyclist's

LAKE DISTRICT AND MORECAMBE BAY

CONISTON COPPER MINES
CUMBRIA WAY & ALLERDALE RAMBLE
THE CHRONICLES OF MILNTHORPE
THE EDEN WAY
FROM FELL AND FIELD
KENDAL - A SOCIAL HISTORY
A LAKE DISTRICT ANGLER"S GUIDE
LAKELAND TOWNS
LAKELAND VILLAGES
LAKELAND PANORAMAS
THE LOST RESORT?
SCRAMBLES IN THE LAKE DISTRICT
MORE SCRAMBLES IN THE LAKE DISTRICT
SHORT WALKS IN LAKELAND
Book 1: SOUTH
Book 2: NORTH
Book 3: WEST
ROCKY RAMBLER'S WILD WALKS
RAIN OR SHINE
ROADS AND TRACKS OF THE LAKE DISTRICT
THE TARNS OF LAKELAND Vol 1: West
THE TARNS OF LAKELAND Vol 2: East
WALKING ROUND THE LAKES
WALKS SILVERDALE/ARNSIDE
WINTER CLIMBS IN LAKE DISTRICT

NORTH-WEST ENGLAND

WALKING IN CHESHIRE
FAMILY WALKS IN FOREST OF BOWLAND
WALKING IN THE FOREST OF BOWLAND
LANCASTER CANAL WALKS
WALKER'S GUIDE TO LANCASTER CANAL
CANAL WALKS VOL 1: NORTH
WALKS FROM THE LEEDS-LIVERPOOL CANAL
THE RIBBLE WAY
WALKS IN RIBBLE COUNTRY
WALKING IN LANCASHIRE
WALKS ON THE WEST PENNINE MOORS
WALKS IN LANCASHIRE WITCH COUNTRY
HADRIAN'S WALL
Vol 1 : The Wall Walk
Vol 2 : Wall Country Walks

NORTH-EAST ENGLAND

NORTH YORKS MOORS
THE REIVER'S WAY
THE TEESDALE WAY
WALKING IN COUNTY DURHAM
WALKING IN THE NORTH PENNINES
WALKING IN NORTHUMBERLAND
WALKING IN THE WOLDS
WALKS IN THE NORTH YORK MOORS Books 1 and 2
WALKS IN THE YORKSHIRE DALES Books 1,2 and 3
WALKS IN DALES COUNTRY
WATERFALL WALKS - TEESDALE & HIGH PENNINES
THE YORKSHIRE DALES
YORKSHIRE DALES ANGLER'S GUIDE

THE PEAK DISTRICT

STAR FAMILY WALKS PEAK DISTRICT/Sth YORKS
HIGH PEAK WALKS
WEEKEND WALKS IN THE PEAK DISTRICT
WHITE PEAK WALKS
Vol.1 Northern Dales
Vol.2 Southern Dales
WHITE PEAK WAY
WALKING IN PEAKLAND
WALKING IN SHERWOOD FORES
WALKING IN STAFFORDSHIRE
THE VIKING WAY

WALES AND WELSH BORDERS

ANGLESEY COAST WALKS
ASCENT OF SNOWDON
THE BRECON BEACONS
CLWYD ROCK
HEREFORD & THE WYE VALLEY
HILLWALKING IN SNOWDONIA
HILLWALKING IN WALES Vol.1
HILLWALKING IN WALES Vol.2
LLEYN PENINSULA COASTAL PATH
WALKING OFFA'S DYKE PATH
THE PEMBROKESHIRE COASTAL PATH
THE RIDGES OF SNOWDONIA
SARN HELEN
SCRAMBLES IN SNOWDONIA
SEVERN WALKS
THE SHROPSHIRE HILLS
THE SHROPSHIRE WAY
SPIRIT PATHS OF WALES
WALKING DOWN THE WYE
A WELSH COAST TO COAST WALK
WELSH WINTER CLIMBS

THE MIDLANDS

CANAL WALKS VOL 2: MIDLANDS
THE COTSWOLD WAY
COTSWOLD WALKS Book 1: North
COTSWOLD WALKS Book 2: Central
COTSWOLD WALKS Book 3: South
THE GRAND UNION CANAL WALK
HEART OF ENGLAND WALKS
WALKING IN OXFORDSHIRE
WALKING IN WARWICKSHIRE
WALKING IN WORCESTERSHIRE
WEST MIDLANDS ROCK

SOUTH AND SOUTH-WEST ENGLAND

WALKING IN BEDFORDSHIRE
WALKING IN BUCKINGHAMSHIRE
CHANNEL ISLAND WALKS
CORNISH ROCK
WALKING IN CORNWALL
WALKING IN THE CHILTERNS
WALKING ON DARTMOOR
WALKING IN DEVON
WALKING IN DORSET
CANAL WALKS VOL 3: SOUTH
EXMOOR & THE QUANTOCKS
THE GREATER RIDGEWAY
WALKING IN HAMPSHIRE
THE ISLE OF WIGHT
THE KENNET & AVON WALK
THE LEA VALLEY WALK
LONDON THEME WALKS
THE NORTH DOWNS WAY
THE SOUTH DOWNS WAY
THE ISLES OF SCILLY
THE SOUTHERN COAST TO COAST
SOUTH WEST WAY
Vol.1 Mineh'd to Penz.
Vol.2 Penz. to Poole
WALKING IN SOMERSET
WALKING IN SUSSEX
THE THAMES PATH
TWO MOORS WAY
WALKS IN KENT Book 1
WALKS IN KENT Book 2
THE WEALDWAY & VANGUARD WAY

SCOTLAND

WALKING IN THE ISLE OF ARRAN
THE BORDER COUNTRY - A WALKERS GUIDE
BORDER COUNTRY CYCLE ROUTES
BORDER PUBS & INNS - A WALKERS' GUIDE
CAIRNGORMS, Winter Climbs 5th Edition

LISTING OF CICERONE GUIDES

CENTRAL HIGHLANDS
6 LONG DISTANCE WALKS
WALKING THE GALLOWAY HILLS
WALKING IN THE HEBRIDES
NORTH TO THE CAPE
THE ISLAND OF RHUM
THE ISLE OF SKYE A Walker's Guide
WALKS IN THE LAMMERMUIRS
WALKING IN THE LOWTHER HILLS
THE SCOTTISH GLENS SERIES
1 - CAIRNGORM GLENS
2 - ATHOLL GLENS
3 - GLENS OF RANNOCH
4 - GLENS OF TROSSACH
5 - GLENS OF ARGYLL
6 - THE GREAT GLEN
7 - THE ANGUS GLENS
8 - KNOYDART TO MORVERN
9 - THE GLENS OF ROSS-SHIRE
SCOTTISH RAILWAY WALKS
SCRAMBLES IN LOCHABER
SCRAMBLES IN SKYE
SKI TOURING IN SCOTLAND
THE SPEYSIDE WAY
TORRIDON - A Walker's Guide
WALKS FROM THE WEST HIGHLAND RAILWAY
THE WEST HIGHLAND WAY
WINTER CLIMBS NEVIS & GLENCOE

IRELAND

IRISH COASTAL WALKS
THE IRISH COAST TO COAST
THE MOUNTAINS OF IRELAND

WALKING AND TREKKING IN THE ALPS

WALKING IN THE ALPS
100 HUT WALKS IN THE ALPS
CHAMONIX to ZERMATT
GRAND TOUR OF MONTE ROSA Vol. 1 and Vol. 2
TOUR OF MONT BLANC

FRANCE, BELGIUM AND LUXEMBOURG

WALKING IN THE ARDENNES
ROCK CLIMBS BELGIUM & LUX.
THE BRITTANY COASTAL PATH
CHAMONIX - MONT BLANC Walking Guide
WALKING IN THE CEVENNES
CORSICAN HIGH LEVEL ROUTE: GR20
THE ECRINS NATIONAL PARK
WALKING THE FRENCH ALPS: GR5
WALKING THE FRENCH GORGES
FRENCH ROCK
WALKING IN THE HAUTE SAVOIE
WALKING IN THE LANGUEDOC
TOUR OF THE OISANS: GR54
WALKING IN PROVENCE
THE PYRENEAN TRAIL: GR10
THE TOUR OF THE QUEYRAS
ROBERT LOUIS STEVENSON TRAIL
WALKING IN TARENTAISE & BEAUFORTAIN ALPS
ROCK CLIMBS IN THE VERDON
TOUR OF THE VANOISE
WALKS IN VOLCANO COUNTRY

FRANCE/SPAIN

ROCK CLIMBS IN THE PYRENEES
WALKS & CLIMBS IN THE PYRENEES
THE WAY OF ST JAMES
Le Puy to Santiago - Walker's
THE WAY OF ST JAMES
Le Puy to Santiago - Cyclist's

SPAIN AND PORTUGAL

WALKING IN THE ALGARVE
ANDALUSIAN ROCK CLIMBS
BIRDWATCHING IN MALLORCA
COSTA BLANCA ROCK
COSTA BLANCA WALKS VOL 1
COSTA BLANCA WALKS VOL 2
WALKING IN MALLORCA
ROCK CLIMBS IN MAJORCA, IBIZA & TENERIFE
WALKING IN MADEIRA
THE MOUNTAINS OF CENTRAL SPAIN
THE SPANISH PYRENEES GR11 2nd Ed.
WALKING IN THE SIERRA NEVADA
WALKS & CLIMBS IN THE PICOS DE EUROPA
VIA DE LA PLATA

SWITZERLAND

ALPINE PASS ROUTE, SWITZERLAND
THE BERNESE ALPS A Walking Guide
CENTRAL SWITZERLAND
THE JURA: HIGH ROUTE & SKI TRAVERSES
WALKING IN TICINO, SWITZERLAND
THE VALAIS, SWITZERLAND. A Walking Guide

GERMANY, AUSTRIA AND EASTERN EUROPE

MOUNTAIN WALKING IN AUSTRIA
WALKING IN THE BAVARIAN ALPS
WALKING IN THE BLACK FOREST
THE DANUBE CYCLE WAY
GERMANY'S ROMANTIC ROAD
WALKING IN THE HARZ MOUNTAINS
KING LUDWIG WAY
KLETTERSTEIG Northern Limestone Alps
WALKING THE RIVER RHINE TRAIL
THE MOUNTAINS OF ROMANIA
WALKING IN THE SALZKAMMERGUT
HUT-TO-HUT IN THE STUBAI ALPS
THE HIGH TATRAS

SCANDANAVIA

WALKING IN NORWAY
ST OLAV'S WAY

ITALY AND SLOVENIA

ALTA VIA - HIGH LEVEL WALKS DOLOMITES
CENTRAL APENNINES OF ITALY
WALKING CENTRAL ITALIAN ALPS
WALKING IN THE DOLOMITES
SHORTER WALKS IN THE DOLOMITES
WALKING ITALY'S GRAN PARADISO
LONG DISTANCE WALKS IN ITALY'S GRAN PARADISO
ITALIAN ROCK
WALKS IN THE JULIAN ALPS
WALKING IN SICILY
WALKING IN TUSCANY
VIA FERRATA SCRAMBLES IN THE DOLOMITES

OTHER MEDITERRANEAN COUNTRIES

THE ATLAS MOUNTAINS
WALKING IN CYPRUS
CRETE - THE WHITE MOUNTAINS
THE MOUNTAINS OF GREECE
JORDAN - Walks, Treks, Caves etc.
THE MOUNTAINS OF TURKEY
TREKS & CLIMBS WADI RUM JORDAN
CLIMBS & TREKS IN THE ALA DAG
WALKING IN PALESTINE

HIMALAYA

ADVENTURE TREKS IN NEPAL
ANNAPURNA - A TREKKER'S GUIDE
EVEREST - A TREKKERS' GUIDE
GARHWAL & KUMAON - A Trekker's Guide
KANGCHENJUNGA - A Trekker's Guide
LANGTANG, GOSAINKUND & HELAMBU Trekkers Guide
MANASLU - A trekker's guide

OTHER COUNTRIES

MOUNTAIN WALKING IN AFRICA - KENYA
OZ ROCK – AUSTRALIAN CRAGS
WALKING IN BRITISH COLUMBIA
TREKKING IN THE CAUCAUSUS
GRAND CANYON & AMERICAN SOUTH WEST
ROCK CLIMBS IN HONG KONG
ADVENTURE TREKS WEST NORTH AMERICA
CLASSIC TRAMPS IN NEW ZEALAND

TECHNIQUES AND EDUCATION

SNOW & ICE TECHNIQUES
ROPE TECHNIQUES
THE BOOK OF THE BIVVY
THE HILLWALKER'S MANUAL
THE TREKKER'S HANDBOOK
THE ADVENTURE ALTERNATIVE
BEYOND ADVENTURE
FAR HORIZONS - ADVENTURE TRAVEL FOR ALL
MOUNTAIN WEATHER

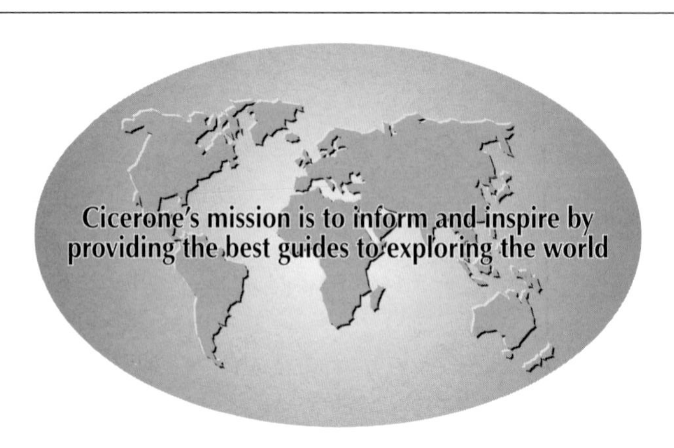

Since its foundation over 30 years ago, Cicerone has specialised in publishing guidebooks and has built a reputation for quality and reliability. It now publishes nearly 300 guides to the major destinations for outdoor enthusiasts, including Europe, UK and the rest of the world.

Written by leading and committed specialists, Cicerone guides are recognised as the most authoritative. They are full of information, maps and illustrations so that the user can plan and complete a successful and safe trip or expedition – be it a long face climb, a walk over Lakeland fells, an alpine traverse, a Himalayan trek or a ramble in the countryside.

With a thorough introduction to assist planning, clear diagrams, maps and colour photographs to illustrate the terrain and route, and accurate and detailed text, Cicerone guides are designed for ease of use and access to the information.

If the facts on the ground change, or there is any aspect of a guide that you think we can improve, we are always delighted to hear from you.

Cicerone Press
2 Police Square Milnthorpe Cumbria LA7 7PY
Tel:01539 562 069 Fax:01539 563 417
e-mail:info@cicerone.co.uk web:www.cicerone.co.uk